I0007505

Prezi HOTSH⊕T

Create amazing Prezi presentations through 10 exciting
Prezi projects

Hedwyg van Groenendaal

BIRMINGHAM - MUMBAI

Prezi HOTSHT

Copyright © 2014 Packt Publishing

All rights reserved. No part of this book may be reproduced, stored in a retrieval system, or transmitted in any form or by any means, without the prior written permission of the publisher, except in the case of brief quotations embedded in critical articles or reviews.

Every effort has been made in the preparation of this book to ensure the accuracy of the information presented. However, the information contained in this book is sold without warranty, either express or implied. Neither the author, nor Packt Publishing, and its dealers and distributors will be held liable for any damages caused or alleged to be caused directly or indirectly by this book.

Packt Publishing has endeavored to provide trademark information about all of the companies and products mentioned in this book by the appropriate use of capitals. However, Packt Publishing cannot guarantee the accuracy of this information.

First published: April 2014

Production Reference: 1180414

Published by Packt Publishing Ltd.
Livery Place
35 Livery Street
Birmingham B3 2PB, UK.

ISBN 978-1-84969-977-8

www.packtpub.com

Cover Image by Peter van Teeseling (pvantees@gmail.com)

Credits

Author
Hedwyg van Groenendaal

Reviewers
Marthe Bijman

Jeremine Holt

David Hopkins

Mikah J. Pritchard

J.J. Sylvia IV

Commissioning Editor
Usha Iyer

Acquisition Editors
Pramila Balan

Meeta Rajani

Content Development Editor
Chalini Snega Victor

Technical Editors
Krishnaveni Haridas

Novina Kewalramani

Anand Singh

Copy Editor
Roshni Banerjee

Project Coordinator
Amey Sawant

Proofreader
Ameesha Green

Indexer
Mariammal Chettiyar

Production Coordinator
Nilesh Bambardekar

Cover Work
Nilesh Bambardekar

About the Author

Hedwyg van Groenendaal (1971, MSc) has 20 years of experience in the field of the Internet and web design. This started during her studies in building Information Technology at Eindhoven University of Technology. She graduated in 1995. Quite soon after finishing her studies, she started her own Internet and web design company called Via Milia, and a few years later, she started an Internet education center.

Hedwyg is passionate about creating easy access to tools and techniques that are (or seem) difficult for many people. She is knowledgeable, enthusiastic, creative, passionate, technical, analytical, and is also an expert in Prezi and social media. Her motto is "If you can't explain it simply, you don't understand it well enough".

Hedwyg has already written 10 books on web design, Flash, ActionScript, and Dreamweaver as well as five books on Prezi (four in Dutch and one in English, *The Ultimate Prezi Guide*). She founded Prezi University. From this initiative, workshops, trainings, seminars and events about Prezi are organized, such as the annual Prezi day.

Prezi.com appreciates all the initiatives by Hedwyg van Groenendaal and decided to appoint her as one of the first official Prezi Experts.

On February 28, 2013, Hedwyg won the worldwide TED-Prezi contest, Ideas Matter, with her Prezi IDENTITY, which was inspired by Bryan Stevenson's TED talk "We need to talk about an injustice".

You will find more information on Hedwyg van Groenendaal and her company, Prezi University, at www.preziuniversity.com, and facebook.com/preziuniversity, and you can also follow her on her Twitter accounts: @hedwygNL and @preziuniversity.

Acknowledgments

I would like to thank my husband Ton, and my children Keyon, Shimara, and Mazon for all their support and enthusiasm during the writing process of this book. You are very important and the best thing that ever happened to me!

Many thanks to my parents, who have always been right behind me my whole life. I deeply appreciate that.

Thank you to all the people from Packt Publishing and the reviewers for the help, the critical notes, and the compliments.

Herinneringen die je later wilt hebben, moet je nu maken.

Create now the memories you want to keep for later.

About the Reviewers

Marthe Bijman is a writer, literary critic, and communications specialist in Mining Engineering. She has worked extensively in the Mining and Information Technology industries. She holds a BA degree, BA Honors in Literature, BA Honors in Journalism, H.Dip.Ed in Language Teaching, and MA in Applied Linguistics and Literary Sciences. She has nurtured a lifelong interest in language and literary analysis, and is an astute and prolific reader and literature reviewer. She publishes her reviews and thoughts on the written word on her blog and website, www.sevencircumstances.com. In collaboration with her husband, she is the author and designer of self-published photography, reference, and poetry books, featured at www.blurb.com. Born in South Africa, she now lives and works in Vancouver, Canada.

Jeremine Holt is a passionate presentation designer, illustrator, and a Prezi trainer. She lives in Rotterdam, Holland and knows how to successfully combine entrepreneurship and being a single mum. Since she started her graphic design business in 1999, she's also been teaching about design software and the design process to students, adults, and children. She is always on the lookout for chances to create authentic visual communication with preferably multiple layers of meaning. Therefore, being just a graphic designer (http://www.westenwindontwerp.nl) wasn't enough. She did elaborate research on visualization methods that can be used to improve the results of change management. Her conclusion is that visualizing change and showing where an organization wants to go and how to get there is very effective. It gets people engaged and motivated.

While looking for the best way to present her visualizations, she discovered Prezi in 2010. She realized that Prezi isn't just a tool. When used in the right way, it can be a motor for creativity, innovation, and visual thinking.

Since then, she's been teaching Prezi and creating visual presentations (http://www.thepreziexperience.nl). Jeremine has, for example, worked for Rotterdam's city manager, for the Dutch Ministry of Infrastructure and Environment, and for the international consultancy firm, Auren.

These days, she's further developing her business in presentation design and visual content creation. It's her mission to build as many bridges as possible between creativity and the business world.

David Hopkins is an experienced and respected Learning Technologist in the UK. His work and research focuses on the use of appropriate technology for students, online and on campus. From a background in commercial Internet technologies and online communities, David has been able to apply knowledge and experience with online learning and support and bring about effective and appropriate use of technology for learning. His current interests and research are based around the use of mobile devices for online learning (for both campus and distance learners), and the use of social media and social networks for effective communication and collaboration between staff, students, and his peers.

David Hopkins is a regular blogger at www.dontwasteyourtime.co.uk. He blogs about different aspects of learning technology, Blackboard, CMS/VLEs, social networks, and other aspects of the utilization of technology in a pedagogic environment. He started blogging about his experiences and activities in 2008, but has been an advocate of blogging and online "communities" since 1999. He first worked as a web designer. Prezi has long been David's passion and he offers Prezi workshops to academic staff and students alike and enables students to leave higher education ready for the modern office environment, giving them skills and knowledge to incorporate new technologies and new approaches to existing technology in the workplace.

Mikah J. Pritchard is an Instructional Designer currently living in Kentucky. She has an MS. Ed. degree in Instructional Systems Technology from Indiana University and has begun working on her Doctorate in Educational Psychology from University of Kentucky. She develops e-learning courses that implement new technologies to produce engaging instruction with a strong theoretical basis. Her passion for graphic design is incorporated into all of her instructional projects.

Mikah has worked at Vincennes University, DePauw University, and is currently working at Eastern Kentucky University. At EKU, she works within the Instructional Development Center (IDC) on course design for e-campus courses. Her areas of expertise include instructional design, instructional technology consulting, graphic design, student support, and social media education.

She has also reviewed *Mastering Prezi for Business*, *Russell Anderson-Williams*, R., *Packt Publishing* (reviewed in 2012 prior to publication).

J.J. Sylvia IV has experience spanning the fields of business, education, and non-profit that have given him the opportunity to develop a unique perspective on the way people use and engage with technology.

As a PhD student in the communication, rhetoric, and digital media program at North Carolina State University, he researches and teaches people about the way technology affects one's view of the world and can be used persuasively for positive change. He has also managed paid advertising and marketing strategies for an e-commerce site, developed a social media outreach initiative for a non-profit, managed AmeriCorps interns who worked to integrate technology into the classroom, and built a community around an educational outreach blog.

J.J. Sylvia IV has published chapters in books such as *Ethical Issues in E-Business*, published by *Business Science Reference*; and *Radiohead and Philosophy*, *Doctor Who and Philosophy*, and *Supervillains and Philosophy*, all published by *Open Court*.

www.PacktPub.com

Support files, eBooks, discount offers and more

You might want to visit www.PacktPub.com for support files and downloads related to your book.

Did you know that Packt offers eBook versions of every book published, with PDF and ePub files available? You can upgrade to the eBook version at www.PacktPub.com and as a print book customer, you are entitled to a discount on the eBook copy. Get in touch with us at service@packtpub.com for more details.

At www.PacktPub.com, you can also read a collection of free technical articles, sign up for a range of free newsletters and receive exclusive discounts and offers on Packt books and eBooks.

http://PacktLib.PacktPub.com

Do you need instant solutions to your IT questions? PacktLib is Packt's online digital book library. Here, you can access, read and search across Packt's entire library of books.

Why Subscribe?

  ▶ Fully searchable across every book published by Packt
  ▶ Copy and paste, print and bookmark content
  ▶ On demand and accessible via web browser

Free Access for Packt account holders

If you have an account with Packt at www.PacktPub.com, you can use this to access PacktLib today and view nine entirely free books. Simply use your login credentials for immediate access.

Table of Contents

Preface

Prezi is an innovative, web-based presentation tool based on an infinite canvas. This canvas and its zooming features are the powers of Prezi. Zooming out provides an overview and, zooming in provides details. You can look at a Prezi presentation as a large mind map. Put text, images, and videos on the canvas and structure your content by frames. Make the important points big and make the details smaller in size. A path in the prezi sets the storyline of the presentation.

Adam Somlai-Fischer invented Prezi in 2007. Adam is originally a media artist and architect, and he felt that the traditional form of slides limited him when he was shaping and drawing up his ideas. He made his first zooming interface in 2001. Together with Peter Halacsy, he started working on an application in 2007 in Budapest, Hungary. They called this tool ZuiPrezi. "Zui" for the Zooming User Interface (ZUI) and Prezi as it is the Hungarian diminutive for presentation. However, very soon they called it Prezi. Peter Arvai joined the team as CEO, and the new presentation tool Prezi was officially launched on April 5, 2009.

This book presents a series of fully realized Prezi projects. It will teach you how to build great prezis. The book builds up on complexity and difficulty. You will not only learn tips and tricks, but also the techniques and workflow used. The ten projects in this book are completely different from each other, and they will give you inspiration and ideas for your own projects. Take a look at www.prezihotshot.com for a sneak preview of the projects.

We hope that you enjoy working on your Prezi projects and may this book inspire you to get the most out of it!

What this book covers

Project 1, *The Fastest Way to Go from an Idea to a Prezi*, teaches you how to create a prezi by using brainstorming techniques. You will learn how to brainstorm in Prezi, how to go from a brainstorm to a mind map, and how to structure your content.

Project 2, *Present Yourself with a Prezumé*, shows you how to present yourself online with a more creative curriculum vitae. A résumé in Prezi is a prezumé!

Project 3, *I Want to Use Prezi for My Lessons*, teaches how you can use Prezi to create learning materials. In this project, we will create a prezi about "The world of bees."

Project 4, *Designing a Serious Corporate Presentation*, helps you to create better business presentations in Prezi by using a seven-step workflow.

Project 5, *Presenting in the PechaKucha Style*, teaches you how to use a whole new way of presenting. You will learn how to build a prezi in PechaKucha style.

Project 6, *Presenting Boring Stuff in a Better Way*, teaches you how to present data in a much better way. The challenge is to make data visually more attractive.

Project 7, *I Really Like Those Hand-drawn Prezis*, shows you it's not difficult to make your own drawings to tell your story in Prezi.

Project 8, *Let's Animate Your Prezi*, teaches you how to create stunning Flash animations and use them in Prezi. You'll create a Prezi machine step by step.

Project 9, *More Interactivity with the Prezi Player API*, teaches you how to create a menu on a website to navigate through your embedded prezi. You'll be using the Prezi Player API.

Project 10, *Creating an Award-winning Prezi*, shows you how the winning prezi IDENTITY of the TED + Prezi Contest, Ideas Matter, was created.

What you need for this book

Of course, you need a Prezi account (www.prezi.com). Any Prezi account will do to create the projects of this book. The Prezi.com website supports all major modern browsers.

You don't need additional software for the first five projects of the book. In the last four projects, we'll be using Microsoft Excel, Adobe Illustrator, Adobe Flash Professional (www.adobe.com/products), and the Prezi Player API (prezi.github.io/prezi-player). You don't need the latest software. GIMP (www.gimp.org) or Inkscape (www.inkscape.org) are an alternative to Adobe Illustrator.

Who this book is for

You know how to make a basic presentation with Prezi. You played around with the tool; you know how to insert text, images, and videos and how to create a path in your prezi. You have seen really cool Prezi presentations online and if you are wondering how they were created, this book is perfect for you.

This book covers 10 different Prezi projects; each project has its own area of focus. You'll learn a lot of practical details and tips. You'll also learn a seven-step workflow that will help you create better presentations and to get the most out of Prezi.

You'll learn how the professionals build their presentations with Prezi with this *Prezi Hotshot* book.

Conventions

A hotshot book has the following sections:

Mission briefing

This section explains what you will build, with a screenshot of the completed project.

Why is it awesome?

This section explains why the project is cool, unique, exciting, and interesting. It describes the advantages the project will give you.

Your Hotshot objectives

This section explains the major tasks required to complete your project, which are as follows:

- Task 1
- Task 2
- Task 3
- Task 4

Mission checklist

This section mentions the prerequisites for the project (if any), such as resources or libraries that need to be downloaded.

Task 1

This section explains the task that you will perform.

Prepare for lift off

This section explains any preliminary work that you may need to do before beginning work on the task.

Engage thrusters

This section lists the steps required in order to complete the task.

Objective complete – mini debriefing

This section explains how the steps performed in the previous section (*Engage thrusters*) allow us to complete the task.

Classified intel

This section provides extra information that is relevant to the task.

After all the tasks are completed, the following sections should appear:

Mission accomplished

This section explains the task we accomplished in the project. This is mandatory and should occur after all the tasks in the project are completed.

A Hotshot challenge / Hotshot challenges

This section explains things to be done or tasks to be performed using the concepts explained in this project.

In this book, you will find a number of styles of text that distinguish between different kinds of information. Here are some examples of these styles, and an explanation of their meaning.

Code words in text, database table names, folder names, filenames, file extensions, pathnames, dummy URLs, user input, and Twitter handles are shown as follows: "We can include other contexts through the use of the `include` directive."

New terms and **important words** are shown in bold. Words that you see on the screen, in menus or dialog boxes for example, appear in the text like this: "Clicking on the **Next** button moves you to the next screen."

Warnings or important notes appear in a box like this.

Tips and tricks appear like this.

Reader feedback

Feedback from our readers is always welcome. Let us know what you think about this book—what you liked or may have disliked. Reader feedback is important for us to develop titles that you really get the most out of.

To send us general feedback, simply send an e-mail to `feedback@packtpub.com`, and mention the book title via the subject of your message.

If there is a topic that you have expertise in and you are interested in either writing or contributing to a book, see our author guide on `www.packtpub.com/authors`.

Customer support

Now that you are the proud owner of a Packt book, we have a number of things to help you to get the most from your purchase.

Downloading the color images of this book

We also provide you a PDF file that has color images of the screenshots/diagrams used in this book. The color images will help you better understand the changes in the output. You can download this file from: `https://www.packtpub.com/sites/default/files/downloads/9778OT_ColoredImages.pdf`

Errata

Although we have taken every care to ensure the accuracy of our content, mistakes do happen. If you find a mistake in one of our books—maybe a mistake in the text or the code—we would be grateful if you would report this to us. By doing so, you can save other readers from frustration and help us improve subsequent versions of this book. If you find any errata, please report them by visiting `http://www.packtpub.com/submit-errata`, selecting your book, clicking on the errata submission form link, and entering the details of your errata. Once your errata are verified, your submission will be accepted and the errata will be uploaded on our website, or added to any list of existing errata, under the Errata section of that title. Any existing errata can be viewed by selecting your title from `http://www.packtpub.com/support`.

Piracy

Piracy of copyright material on the Internet is an ongoing problem across all media. At Packt, we take the protection of our copyright and licenses very seriously. If you come across any illegal copies of our works, in any form, on the Internet, please provide us with the location address or website name immediately so that we can pursue a remedy. Please contact us at `copyright@packtpub.com` with a link to the suspected pirated material. We appreciate your help in protecting our authors, and our ability to bring you valuable content.

Questions

You can contact us at `questions@packtpub.com` if you are having a problem with any aspect of the book, and we will do our best to address it.

Project 1

The Fastest Way to Go from an Idea to a Prezi

Using the brainstorming techniques in Prezi, it is easy to create a good prezi. We will go from brainstorming to a mind map and use that as a basis for our prezi.

Mission briefing

In this project, we will create a Prezi presentation based on just an idea. Often, people have an idea for a presentation they have to build, but they don't have any idea about what the exact content should be. They end up including a lot of details and are not able to build a clear structure for their presentation.

A good presentation consists of a clear message, a few main topics, and a clear structure for all the information.

Brainstorming is ideal to generate ideas and content (diverge), but don't forget to mark the main ideas and get rid of the information you don't really need (converge). Divergent thinking is about expanding your ideas, looking for alternatives, quantity, trial and error, chaos, and intuition. With divergent thinking, you can explore as many aspects of a concept as possible. Convergent thinking is about focus, selecting ideas, choosing, structuring, organizing, quality, and logic. Convergent thinking is the opposite of divergent thinking.

It's important to create a distinction between the main topics and the details. Ideally, you should have three main topics. That's enough. Not all information is of the same importance. You'll have main topics, subtopics, and details. The result of our structuring session is a clear mind map (in Prezi!) that we will use as a basis for our presentation in Prezi.

Using a mind map for your Prezi presentation is the easiest way to use Prezi in a good way. This way of presenting always works, because you zoom in for the details and zoom out for the overview.

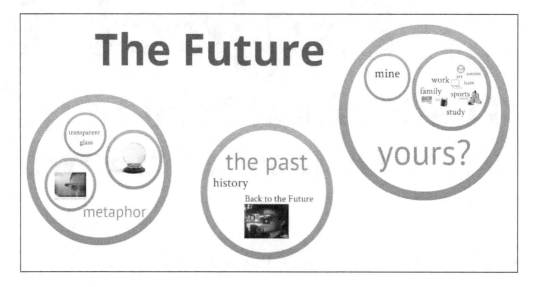

Why is it awesome?

Brainstorming is a great way to develop the content for your presentation. Put your brains to work and you will be able to come up with the best and creative ideas. Yes, you too can be creative! It's easy. Just follow this project and you'll learn to generate ideas in Prezi and create a great prezi out of it.

We'll also keep you from falling into the trap of trying to brainstorm and structure at the same time, as that would just complicate things. In this project, you will learn how to first diverge, converge, and finally fill in the details.

Your Hotshot objectives

The major tasks necessary to complete this project are as follows:

- You have an idea, but where do you start?
- Brainstorming in Prezi
- From brainstorming to mind mapping
- Filling in the details
- How should you present your mind map?

Mission checklist

We have no special needs for this project. We'll keep it fast and simple, and we'll be only using Prezi.

The only thing we need to start off is an idea. To make sure that we focus on the process and not too much on the subject itself, we decided to choose a *light* subject for this project. The subject should trigger your brain so that ideas start popping up immediately. Our first idea is to create a presentation about "The Future". This should give you some inspiration!

What about goal, message, and audience? If you think we are forgetting something in the process of creating a presentation, you could be right. Every presentation should start with the following three questions in order to define the goal, message, and audience of the presentation:

- ▸ What do I want to achieve with this presentation? (goal)
- ▸ What do I want the audience to remember? (message)
- ▸ Who is the audience?

Most people never ask these questions and immediately start creating and designing their presentation. If you are not asking yourself what the goal of your presentation is, and if you don't define it, you can never meet that goal and your presentation might never be a success.

However, the focus of this project is on brainstorming, mind mapping, and being creative; therefore, we will not ask these questions yet. The aim of this project is to practice brainstorming and structuring and therefore, we will leave out these three very important questions.

You can look at this project as a free presentation assignment to practice presenting. This could not only be a project for school, but also for the company or organization in which you work. In this project, we'll start with the brainstorming and we'll define our goal, message, and audience later.

You have an idea but where do you start?

We use our idea "The Future" as a starting point for our presentation. We could immediately start in Prezi, but sometimes it's better not to start directly with a computer. First, we need to free our mind.

Engage thrusters

Before you start brainstorming, it's a good idea to free your mind and get ready for some creativity. Pick one task from the following list. Choose the one you never do (or do the least).

- Stand up and take a five-minute walk
- Listen to the sounds around you really carefully for five minutes
- Sing your favorite song from your childhood
- Empty your Lego box on the table and start building something
- Play a game of darts or pool
- Watch a funny YouTube movie
- Run around crazily for one minute
- Laugh out loud for at least one full minute
- Buy and eat an ice cream

Objective complete – mini debriefing

Starting your brainstorm is like preparing for a new task. Brainstorming is fun but also requires hard work. Make sure you are in the right mood, free your mind, and stay focused. You don't have to be relaxed to be creative as a lot of people think, you need to be active.

Now you're ready to start your brainstorm in Prezi.

Brainstorming in Prezi

Let's start brainstorming in Prezi.

Prepare for lift off

Open a new prezi, choose a blank template, and delete all the objects on the canvas. Make sure your canvas is completely empty before you start brainstorming as shown in the next screenshot:

Of course, you can delete the frame by clicking on it and deleting it, but you can also use the key combination *Ctrl + A* and press *Backspace* on your keyboard.

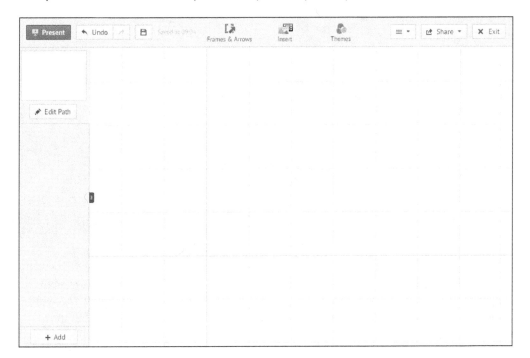

Engage thrusters

We will start our brainstorm by putting our first idea on the canvas. So, click on the canvas and type `The Future`. Make sure the text style is **Body**.

A few ideas will probably start popping up in your mind immediately. Type these ideas on the canvas. It doesn't matter where you put these ideas on the canvas. However, it is preferable if you don't put them too close to each other and definitely not in a straight line.

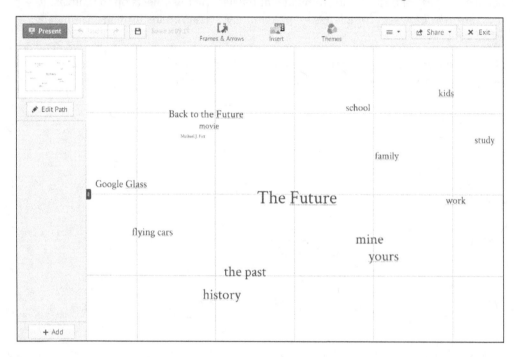

It's important to know that everything that pops up in your mind is okay. It's okay to put everything on the canvas. It's not yet the time to decide if a word is okay or not. The word popped up in your mind, so it's okay. It's that simple and no one should judge that, not even you.

Make use of the infinite canvas of Prezi. The canvas is larger than you think. If the area looks full, pan the canvas (click on the canvas and drag it) to create more room.

At a certain moment, one word may attract your attention. Zoom in to that word (using the plus sign at the right side of the screen), forget the first idea, and start brainstorming about that word—just that word. We zoomed in to the word **history**. When you're done, zoom out by clicking on the small house at the right side of the screen and continue brainstorming, or you can zoom in to another word and start brainstorming about that word.

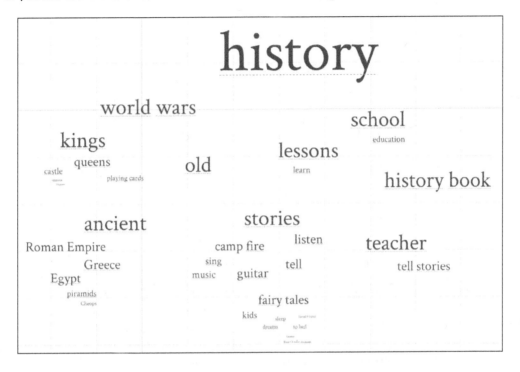

Let this process continue for as long as you want. It's okay to stop for a while or to continue a whole day.

You shouldn't go looking for images or videos as that would break your creativity. If you think of an image, just put the word that the image describes on the canvas.

One last important thing: make the important words big and the details small. You can play around with this and just follow your feeling. The words of the main topics don't have to be of the same height. If one main topic is a bit more important than another main topic, make that first main topic a bit bigger. People will immediately understand that because they see it. They might not be aware of it, but their eyes (actually their brains) see what's more important.

Your final brainstorm could look like the following screenshot:

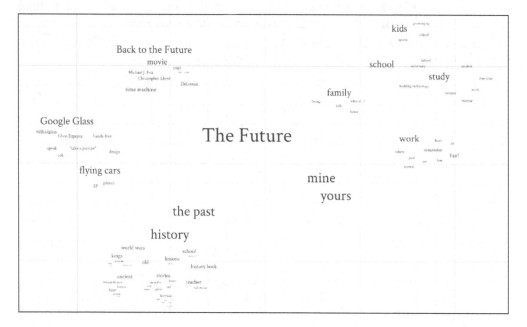

Objective complete – mini debriefing

In this task, we made our first brainstorm in Prezi. First, we put our initial idea on the canvas and then we just started typing words that popped up in our mind. The most important thing of this process is that everything you type is okay. Later on, you can decide which words will stay and which words need to be removed. Sometimes, you zoom into a word and continue brainstorming on just that word. The bigger a word, the more important that word is to you. The main goal of this task is to let the words flow.

Classified intel

When people are creating their presentation, they try to do all things at the same time: think of the content, fill in the content, design the presentation, think of the story to tell, and create the presentation. That doesn't work. These are different processes. You should handle one process at a time. When you are thinking of the content, don't try to design your presentation; similarly, when you are thinking of the story to tell don't try to fill in the content. So, when you are brainstorming, just brainstorm. Don't try to think about how the presentation should look like; that's a different process.

From brainstorm to mind map

Our next task is to turn our brainstorm into a useful mind map. In this process, we need to structure our information, get rid of the information we don't need, and decide which topics will be our main topics. When we limit the number of main topics to three, we'll reach the core of our information.

Engage thrusters

First, we will mark our starting point in our brainstorm (the first idea and our temporary title) and the main topics. We'll use the Prezi text styles for this.

Double-click on the first idea **The Future**, choose the text style **Title**, and make this text big (if it's not already big enough). Use the bigger **A** in the menu to enlarge the text or click on the small circle in the bottom-right corner of the text box as shown in the following screenshot:

Resizing text

You have two options to resize text: inside the text box (editing mode) or via the transformation tool. If you are inside the text box (by double-clicking on the text), you can resize the text by using the small or bigger **A** or the small circle in the bottom-right corner of the text box. Click on the text box once and use the transformation tool to resize the text. The plus sign is used to enlarge the text and the minus sign is used to minimize the text. You can also click-and-drag the small blue squares at the corner of the text box to resize text.

Now, choose your three most important words from all the words on the canvas. These will become your main topics. Double-click on these words and choose the text style **Subtitle** for them. Make these words bigger, but not as big as the title. This is shown in the following screenshot:

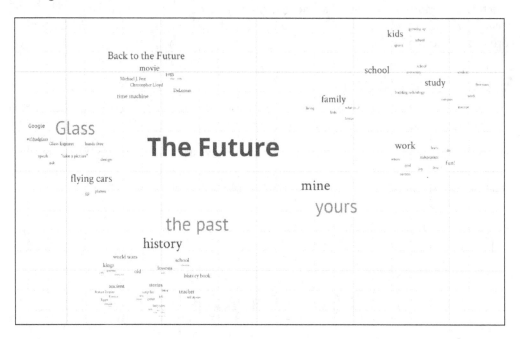

The next step is the most interesting one. For every other word on the canvas, decide whether it should be part of one of our main topics or remove the word. If a word is part of a main topic, move the word to that main topic. If new words pop up in your mind, it's okay to add them to the canvas.

When you finish this process, your canvas will look like the following screenshot. This is the information structure (or mind map) that will be the basis of your presentation.

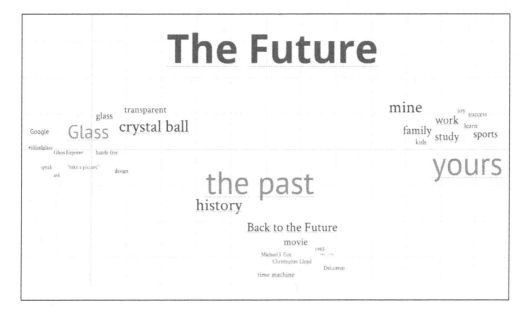

To show relations or to emphasize information, you can add arrows and lines or use the highlighter. This helps you to structure the information further and determine the objects on which you want to focus. It can also help you think about the flow of the information during your presentation.

Arrows and lines are for when you want to show relationships and associations. The highlighter is suitable when you want to emphasize any information. You can even make small drawings with the highlighter. Finally, for extra accentuation, you can also use an arrow that will point at the information, just like the red arrow that is shown in the following screenshot.

 Creating a double-sided arrow is not a standard option in Prezi. So, if you need it, you have to create it yourself by using two separate arrows and putting them next to each other.

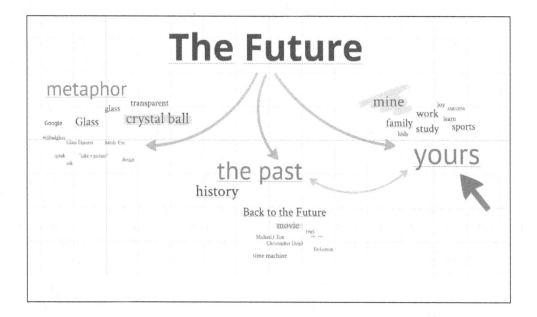

Objective complete – mini debriefing

In this task, you learned how to turn your brainstorm into a mind map. You used **Title** for the subject and **Subtitle** for the three main topics. Our subject is **The Future**, our main topics are **metaphor**, **the past**, and **yours**.

Then, you decided for every other word whether it's a part of a main topic or it should be removed. It's an interesting process and a few new words might pop up in your mind. In our case, the word **metaphor** popped up during our process. A metaphor is a way of describing a subject as something else to make a stronger visual. We will be using a **crystal ball** as a metaphor for **The Future**.

The result of this process is a mind map for your presentation. You can use arrows, lines, and a highlighter to create relationships or emphasize information.

Classified intel

You can take your information structure a step further by using frames. Frames are a great way to visualize a structure. You can use frames to group content, so that if you move a frame, the entire content will move as well. This will enable you to rearrange the information really fast just by moving the frames. Not on paper and not even with post-its can you move information this easily. Use frames in frames to show subtopics and more detailed information.

Frames do not have to be of the same size. You can resize them in the same way as you resize text. The bigger a frame, the more important the information.

Our mind map would look like the following screenshot if we use frames:

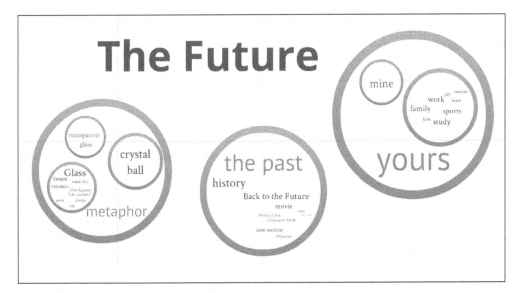

Filling in the details

The most important work for our presentation is done. Just fill in the details and present them. Piece of cake!

Prepare for lift off

What does *filling in the details* exactly mean? It's more than adding a few pictures to your prezi. It's a good idea to use images in your presentation, because you don't have to show in words what you tell. A picture can represent the exact meaning of the things you say, but it can also be a metaphor or a funny picture. Humor is great for presentations.

You don't have to use a picture for every word. Sometimes, you will use a combination of pictures and words. It's important to remember not to show too much at once. Most of the times, it's best to show just one picture or just one word.

Videos also work very well for presentations, because videos can put emotion in the presentations. They also create a quiet moment for you in the presentation when you can think of your next sentences or relax a bit.

So, have a look at your mind map in your prezi and go look for nice pictures and videos. Of course, you can take pictures and videos yourself, but you can also find a lot on the Internet. Make sure you don't violate any copyright laws. If you're not sure, don't use it. There are lots of stock photo sites out there where you can buy (cheap) fantastic material. We bought some pictures from `iStockphoto.com`.

Engage thrusters

As a metaphor for the future, we bought a nice picture of a crystal ball. It's a nice effect to show the crystal ball not in the beginning of the presentation but at the end—as a surprise. We'll start the presentation with our title **The Future**.

We are going from mind map to story. So, let's write down the flow of our presentation first.

We'll start with the text **The Future**. To make a jump to the past, but with a relation to the future, we'll show a small part of the famous movie *Back to the Future*. A few seconds is enough to start our presentation in a nice manner. Then, we'll talk a bit about the future, we'll show a picture of Google Glass, and we'll ask the audience what comes up in their mind when they think about the future. Next, we'll tell about our idea of future and how we think about our family, work, study, and sports in the future. We'll use this as an example for the audience. Then, we'll show the crystal ball as a metaphor because we can't predict the future. Finally, we'll ask the audience to think about their future. We could also ask the audience to grab a piece of paper and write it down to make the presentation more active.

Now, it's time for us to write down the answers to the three important questions we haven't answered yet:

- What do I want to achieve with this presentation? (goal)
- What do I want the audience to remember? (message)
- Who is the audience?

The answers are as follows:

- My personal goal is to create a better presentation using brainstorming techniques and to make the audience more active during my presentation.

▶ I want the audience to say after my presentation, "This wasn't a boring presentation at all. It was actually really nice!"

▶ My colleagues are the audience.

This is how we create the prezi. We'll start by explaining how we made the beginning and the end of the prezi.

What is a path?

With a path you create your storyline in Prezi. You can add every object to the path. When presenting, Prezi automatically zooms in to the objects you added to the path and puts them straight. Your path is the flow of your presentation. You can test your path with the **Present** button. You can click through it with the arrow keys or by using a remote.

To add an object to the path, you first open the path by clicking on the **Edit Path** button on the left-hand side of the screen. Then, just click on the object you want to add to the path and Prezi automatically adds the object to the path. A thumbnail appears for every step in the path. You can drag the thumbnails to change to order of the path.

Creating path step 1 and the end

The following steps show how to create the path step 1 and the last part of the presentation:

1. Insert a image of a crystal ball in your prezi.

2. Make it big and place the crystal ball under the mind map. You can also work inside the mind map. However, because this is the most important picture for the presentation and it's the end point of the prezi, we'll start a new prezi under the mind map.

3. Move (or copy) the text **The Future** inside the ball. Then, put the text **yours** under the crystal ball.

The crystal ball will be the last image of the presentation (zooming out) with an extra zooming out (extra surprise) the text **yours?** will become visible. Let's test this first.

Invisible frames

With frames, you can visually structure the content. This provides your audience with clarity and overview. Frames are also the stepping stones of the path you create to go through your prezi. However, sometimes you don't want all your frames to be visible, because a visible frame can also distract the audience. Then, you can create invisible frames. It works the same as the visible frames, but you don't see these frames in the presentation mode.

You create an invisible frame by selecting **Draw Invisible Frame** from **Frames & Arrows** and then clicking-and-dragging the frame on the canvas.

▸ Draw an invisible frame around the crystal ball

▸ Draw an extra invisible frame around the crystal ball and the text **yours?**.

▸ Add the text **The Future** and the two invisible frames to the path

▸ Test the path via the **Present** button

In the following screenshot, you'll see the path we've made so far in the **Edit Path** side bar on the left-hand side of the screen:

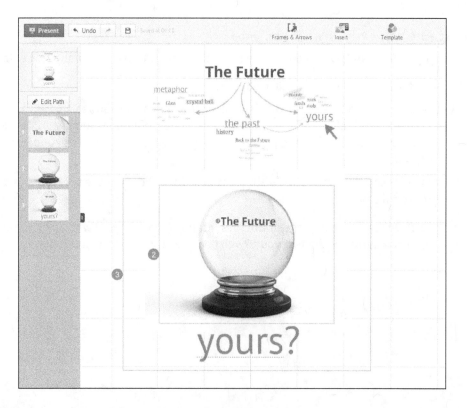

The beginning and the end of the presentation are ready. Now it's time to fill in the middle part.

Creating path step 2

The following steps should be performed to create path step 2:

1. Go to YouTube.com, search for "back to the future" and look for a nice fragment of video.

2. Copy the address of the YouTube movie and return to your prezi.

3. Navigate to **Insert | YouTube video...** and paste the address of the video in the text field.

4. Make the video smaller with the transformation tool to make it fit inside the character **F**.

5. Before you zoom out, add the video to the path and move it to path step two, as shown in the following screenshot:

Creating path step 3

The following steps should be performed to create path step 3:

1. Zoom out completely by clicking on the small house on the right side of the screen.

2. Navigate to **Insert | Image**, type `google glass` in the search field, and mark the checkbox **Search only images licensed for commercial use**, as shown in the following screenshot:

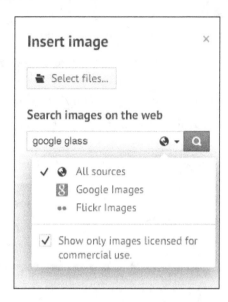

3. Choose a picture and drag it on the canvas.

4. Most of the pictures you'll find in this way are pictures from Wikipedia. To make sure that we are allowed to use this picture, we also search for this picture on the Internet using the query `google glass wikipedia`. We find the source of this picture, read the license, and add the source to the picture.

5. Add the picture to the path and move it to path step 3.

Creating path step 4

The following steps should be performed to create path step 4:

1. Now, copy (or move) the text of the main topic **mine** into the crystal ball. We then change the word **mine** to **my future**.

2. Draw an invisible frame around all these words and add it to the path.

3. Move it to path step 4.

Other path steps

To make our personal story more lively, we add a few pictures and a video to it. We also use some Prezi symbols (the computer and the smiley). You can find these symbols by navigating to **Insert | Symbols & shapes...**. We used the category **Stickers**.

For the section **family**, we copy two photo frames from a Prezi scrapbook template. To do this, perform the following steps:

1. Add a new tab in your browser by using the *Ctrl/Command + T* keys.

2. Find the scrapbook template on `www.prezihotshot.com`, open it in the new tab, and make a copy of this prezi by clicking on the button **Make a copy**. The scrapbook prezi will be copied to your account.

3. Open the prezi in the editor by clicking on the **Edit** button.

4. Select a photo frame and use the *Ctrl/Command + C* keys to copy it.

5. Click on the tab of your original prezi and paste the copied photo frame in it with *Ctrl/Command + V*.

Sometimes, we add the pictures or text directly to the path. We first draw an invisible frame around it and then add the invisible frame to the path, as shown in the following screenshot:

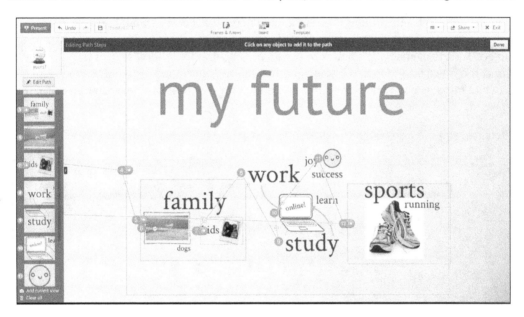

Of course, we need to remove our mind map from the canvas. The fastest way to remove the mind map is to hold down the *Shift* key and click and drag a rectangle around the mind map. Then, click on the *Delete* key.

You can also keep it in a separate prezi file if you want to save it. First, select the mind map by dragging a rectangle around it while holding down the *Shift* key. Then, copy the mind map with *Ctrl/Command + C*. Open a new prezi and paste the mind map in it with *Ctrl/Command + V*.

Our story in prezi is now complete. Watch it online at `www.prezihotshot.com`.

Objective complete – mini debriefing

We went from a brainstorm with lots of words to a prezi with images, video, and a few words. In this task, we finally created our prezi.

We started with a nice image of a crystal ball. We started the prezi and made the last part of the prezi first. The crystal ball is the surprise at the end of the prezi.

Then, we filled in the content of our presentation. We used images and videos and created a nice flow.

Classified intel

If you use frames, it's even easier to fill in the details of your presentation and create a path. You can use the frame-based mind map as the basis and you can leave it as it is. You can only add pictures and videos to it and create a path.

Draw an invisible frame around the whole mind map and add this frame between every main topic in the path. This gives your audience an overview before you go to the next subject. For the overview, it's better to use an invisible frame; otherwise, this frame would attract too much attention and it also would bound the information too much. Now, the structure remains open and there's more attention for the three visible circle frames that represent the subjects.

Of course, you can also watch this prezi online at www.prezihotshot.com.

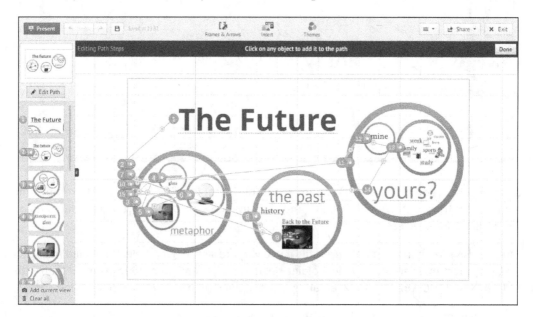

How should you present your mind map?

A lot of people present their prezi online. That's okay as long as you have a good and stable Internet connection. If you do not have a good Internet connection or if you're not sure about doing this, you better download your prezi for your presentation.

Engage thrusters

It doesn't matter which Prezi account you have. You can download your prezi and present it offline with any type of account. The YouTube videos you have added to your prezi cannot be played if you don't have an Internet connection. These movies are not inserted in to your prezi, it's a link to the YouTube movie. Other movies, which can be inserted by selecting **From file (PDF, Video)...** under **Insert**, will always play even without an Internet connection.

In your prezis, go to the prezi you want to download and click on the **Download** button. Click on **Presenting** (the one on the left-hand side) and then click on the **Download** button, as shown in the following screenshot. A ZIP file will download to your computer. This ZIP file contains everything you need to present, for both Windows and Mac. You don't need a browser and there is a built-in Flash Player.

Unzip the ZIP file and double-click on **Prezi.exe** if you are presenting on a Windows machine. The other prezi file is to present on a Mac.

The file will automatically open in the Flash Player. Click on the **Fullscreen** button in the bottom-right corner to show the prezi on a fullscreen as shown in the following screenshot. Now, you are ready to present!

If you want, you can use a remote to click through your presentation instead of using the keyboard arrows. A remote looks much more professional.

 Both the iPad and iPhone don't support Flash. However, you can download the free Prezi apps for both iPad and iPhone. Visit the links `prezi.com/ipad/` and `prezi.com/iphone/` for more information.

Objective complete – mini debriefing

In this task, we explained how you can present your prezi without an Internet connection. It's okay to present online, but your Internet connection must be stable and have enough bandwidth. If it's not working well, it might slow down your presentation and lead to frustration both for you and your audience.

Mission accomplished

We started our presentation with just our first idea and we used the brainstorming technique to generate ideas for our presentation. We were concentrating on thinking up new ideas and generating content. Brainstorming is about diverging.

In the next step, we marked our title and the three main topics and also created the structure of our information. This is about converging information. For every word, we decided whether it was a part of one of the main topics or whether we should get rid of it.

The result of these steps was a clear mind map and information structure. We used it as the basis for our presentation. The last step was the filling in of details and getting ready to present it.

A Hotshot challenge

Now, you've seen how you can brainstorm and develop a structure in Prezi and create a presentation to practice these skills. Choose one of the following subjects, start your brainstorm, create a mind map, fill it with information, and present it to your friends and family!

- ▶ My ideal house
- ▶ When I dream, I think of...
- ▶ My favorite food
- ▶ When I'm old...
- ▶ On an extra day off, I'll...

Project 2
Present Yourself with a Prezumé

Prezi is a great way to create an affective online curriculum vitae to present yourself. In this project, you will learn how you can do that and sell yourself in a more creative way.

The logic is this: résumé + Prezi = prezumé!

Mission briefing

You need a job. How do you present yourself? The same as everyone else, with a boring cover letter that is just a list of facts? Or, do you want to give it a personal touch? Do you want to show a bit more of you? Prezi gives you the opportunity to tell a story—your story.

In this project, we will create a prezumé from start to finish. Our first task is to define our goal, the job we're applying for, and the message we want to tell. Then, the second task will be to gather all the information we might need. Maybe you won't use all the information in our prezumé, but it's better to skip a few things than get short on information. After that, as the third step, we will need to create a clear structure and choose what we want to use in our prezumé. Our fourth task will be to get creative and start thinking of a nice drawing, picture, metaphor, or other creative concepts to use. Then, we have to create our prezumé in Prezi. Finally, we have to share your prezumé to let the world know you are available and looking for a job.

If you follow our guidelines, not only will your job application stand out, but also you will stand out.

Why is it awesome?

The days of boring résumés are over. The standard format is gone and résumés have become more and more visual. On the Internet, there are new tools popping up and some people don't even need such a tool to create a interesting and creative résumé.

Prezi wasn't invented to create résumés but people started using Prezi that way and they called their résumé a prezumé. Prezi is great for storytelling and storytelling is great for your résumé. It's better to tell a story with some highlights than showing a list of all your skills and job experiences.

If you want to stand out in your job search and leave a lasting impression, create a prezumé. We'll show you how.

Your Hotshot objectives

The major tasks to complete this project are as follows:

- ▶ What's your goal?
- ▶ Gathering all the information
- ▶ Structuring and choosing content

- Getting creative!
- Creating your prezumé from start to finish
- Sharing your prezumé

Mission checklist

The only special requirements for this project are that you should be looking for a job, you are sick of boring résumés, and you are ready for something new.

What's your goal?

Before you start creating your prezumé, you should know what job you are applying for, what message you want to tell with your prezumé, and what the goal of your prezumé is.

Prepare for lift off

If you already know what kind of job you're looking for, you can skip this part. If you have no idea, you should first make up your mind and think about this. So, take a break, close your eyes, and visualize what kind of job you would love to have. Here are a few things you can think about:

- Do you want to work for a small company or a multinational company?
- How many hours do you want to work?
- What do you want to do during your working day?
- Do you want to manage or do work?
- How far are you prepared to travel?
- What is your passion and what makes you happy?

Engage thrusters

When you know what job you're looking for, let's put it on paper. Follow the steps listed here:

1. Grab a piece of paper, draw two lines on the paper to divide it into three parts, and write the words "JOB", "MESSAGE", and "GOAL" in the three sections.

2. Start with the "JOB" section. Write down the job you are applying for, at least the job title. If you want, you can add some additional information.

3. Then, write down the message you want to tell in the "MESSAGE" section. This could be "Design is my passion and I want to make it my profession."

4. Finally, write down the goal you want to achieve with your prezumé in the "GOAL" section, for instance "I want the reader to contact me via e-mail to make an appointment for a job interview."

Your piece of paper should look like the following image:

Objective complete – mini debriefing

We made a start with our prezumé on a piece of paper. We divided the paper in three sections and wrote down the job we want, our message, and the goal of our prezumé. Later on, when we are creating our prezumé, we should regularly look back to this piece of paper and check whether we're still on the right track.

Classified intel

If you don't like paper, you could complete this task in Prezi or another tool. The advantage of paper is you can stick it to your wall, so you won't forget about your goal and ambition while you're creating your prezumé. Of course, you could save your prezi as PDF and print it as well.

Gathering all the information

Now that we know what we are aiming for, it's time to gather all the information we need to create our prezumé.

Prepare for lift off

You might already have an extensive LinkedIn profile. That's fantastic, because then you are half way there. If you already have a written résumé, dig it up and use that as a basis. If you have nothing yet, just move on.

Engage thrusters

Usually a résumé is a complete overview of your career so far, including your personal information, special interests, and other things that are relevant to share with your future employer.

Writing your résumé

Before you choose what to put in your prezumé and what to leave out, it's best to collect all the information. If you change your goal in the future, you can still use that document as a basis because it's complete. It might take some time to write down everything, but it's worthwhile and if you keep it up to date, it will be useful for the rest of your life.

An overview of common contents of a résumé is given in the following list:

▸ **Personal data and contact details**: List your full name, gender, date of birth, address, telephone number, e-mail address, and relevant social media pages LinkedIn, Facebook, and Twitter.

▸ **Education**: Starting with the most recent, list the name of the program, name of the school, and the year of graduation. Add trainings and courses as well.

▸ **Work experience**: Starting with the most recent, list the job title, company, city, and year of employment.

▸ **Interesting projects you worked on**: These could be school projects or business projects. If they are of special meaning for your talents, add them to your résumé.

▸ **Skills**: List software skills, management skills, social skills, languages you speak /read/write, and other relevant skills.

▸ **Special interests**: Include personal interests such as hobbies, volunteering, and traveling.

Put all the information in a digital document. If you need examples, just search the Internet for résumé and you'll find lots of examples.

Collecting visual material

Although you've your written résumé ready, you're not finished yet. Now, you are going to collect your visual material, so consider the following:

- A professional photo of yourself.

- If you're a designer, collect proof of your work in the form of photographs, graphics, illustrations, and videos. Build your digital portfolio.

- Proof of your most interesting and relevant projects, such as documents, screen shots, pictures, and videos.

- Collect high-resolution logos of companies where you've worked, especially if they are well-known companies; the logos will look nice in your prezumé.

Objective complete – mini debriefing

In this task, we gathered all the content for our prezumé—both written and visual material. Maybe it was time consuming, but it was absolutely worthwhile because it's the basis for your successful career and future.

Structuring and choosing content

In this task, we will structure the content we have gathered and choose what we really need for our prezumé. This prezumé aims for a specific job; if you want to change jobs in the future, you need to make another prezume.

Prepare for lift off

Make sure you have the paper where you wrote your job, message, and goal; your written and printed résumé; and a highlighter ready.

Engage thrusters

Take a new look at the paper where you wrote your job, message, and goal, grab the highlighter, and mark in your résumé what's really important to include in your prezumé for this specific job application. You don't want to include everything, because then your prezumé would probably become too large. Your prezumé should be short and engaging enough to attract companies to contact you.

The structuring part of this task is automatically done by the categories of your résumé.

Objective complete – mini debriefing

We have chosen the most important parts of our résumé that will be included in our prezumé. This doesn't seem to be a difficult task, but it's an extremely important task. Make sure you pay enough attention to this task.

Getting creative!

Prezi is a creative tool. Use this to become creative yourself and design a beautiful prezumé in Prezi. In this task, we'll inspire you to design your prezumé and we'll give you lots of examples.

Engage thrusters

Before you start thinking about the design of your own prezumé, you should first watch other prezumés and get inspired. Here are three nice examples, you'll also find them online on www.prezihotshot.com. You will find other examples in the **Explore** section on Prezi.com. Just search for prezume and you'll find thousands of prezumés.

Examples

The first example is a prezumé in a loose layout, complete with coffee stains as shown in the following screenshot:

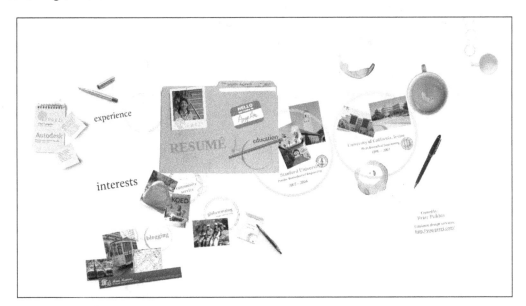

The second example is the story of Mandi Lindner told in a very nice way! It's build up with the subjects iLearn, iAdapt, and iGrow via iProduce and iWill, and ends with iCan in the overview, as shown in the following screenshot:

The last example is the impressive prezumé of Krista Moroder, Director of Learning for Instructional Technology & Library Media for the Kettle Moraine School District in Wisconsin, as shown in the following screenshot:

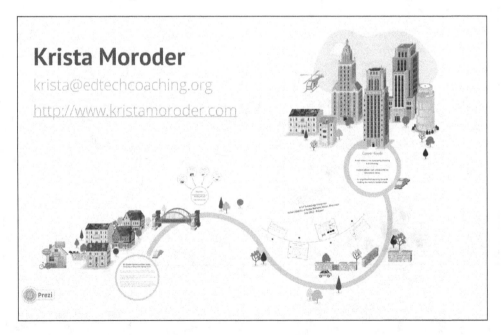

Creative ideas

Of course, there are lots of ideas you can use for your prezumé, maybe the following ideas will help you to create your own unique design:

▸ Use a timeline to list your education, job experience, and skills in a chronological order.

▸ Use a book as a metaphor for your prezumé—*the book of you*.

▸ Instead of a book, you could use a whiteboard, desktop, computer, plain paper, or a company building as a metaphor for your prezumé. A lot of other metaphors are possible depending on the job you are searching.

▸ Create a poster.

▸ Use a really cool image that expresses your passion.

▸ Use your photograph as the basis for your prezumé. This doesn't work for all job applications because you might emphasize yourself too much.

▸ Use your name and put all the information. You literally dive into *your* life to show what your skills and experiences are. You can do the same with the job you want and the name (or logo) of the company where you want to work.

▸ Use an infographic style for your prezumé. There are lots of nice symbols available in Prezi for this.

Using templates

If you find it hard to find a good creative idea for your prezumé, just use a template. `Prezi.com` has three nice templates available that you can use right away.

▸ The first template is a timeline to present your career in a chronological way as shown in the following screenshot:

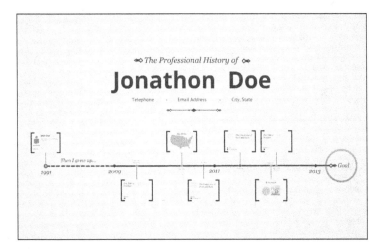

▸ The second template is an example of a desktop, a perfect way to show your skills and experience, as shown in the following screenshot:

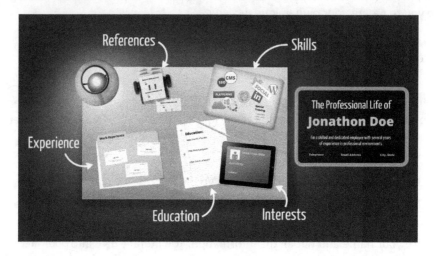

▸ The third template example is a whiteboard with a lot of space to show your creativity, as shown in the following screenshot:

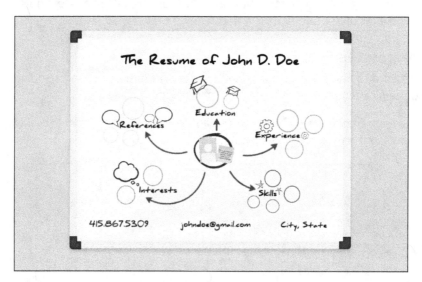

 Find these templates on www.prezihotshot.com.

Objective complete – mini debriefing

You don't have to reinvent the wheel, just get inspired by other prezumés and learn from them. In this task, we gave you lots of creative ideas so that you can create your own unique idea. It's totally okay to steal one of our ideas or to use a Prezi template.

Creating your prezumé from start to finish

Finally, we are ready to create our prezumé in Prezi. This is the most fun part!

Prepare for lift off

For our prezi, we'll use the Scrapbook template of `Prezi.com`. You'll find the link to this template at `www.prezihotshot.com`. You'll also need the paper where you wrote your job, message, and goal, as well asyour résumé with the most important parts highlighted and your visual material.

Engage thrusters

The following steps should be performed to create your prezumé in Prezi:

1. Make a copy of the **Scrapbook** prezi and click on **Edit** to open the prezi, as shown in the following screenshot:

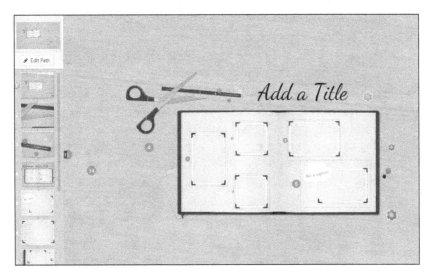

Let's get rid of the things we don't need.

2. Click on the **Edit Path** button and choose **Clear All** to remove the existing path. We'll create our own path later.

3. Then, remove the things that are already in and around the scrapbook, such as the scissors, the flowers, the buttons, and the photo frames. We'll leave one photo frame in the scrapbook for our photograph, as shown in the following screenshot. For now, you can leave the assets in the right-hand side corner of the canvas. You might need these later.

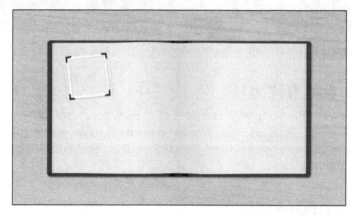

Now, we have an almost empty scrapbook and we can start filling it.

4. First, insert our photograph by navigating to **Insert | Image**. Resize and rotate the picture to fit it in the photo frame. If it's on top of the frame, use the right mouse button and click on **Send Backward** till your photo is between the scrapbook and the photo frame. Do not use **Send to Back** because then it will disappear behind the scrapbook.

5. Maybe you have to crop the picture for an exact fit in the photo frame. Click on the image once, choose **Crop Image**, and drag the corners till the image has the right size.

6. Type in the details of your education, work experience, and skills on the canvas. Choose the **Subtitle** style for these texts. Then, type your name and make your name as big as the other text by dragging the round handle in the right bottom corner. If you see a blue square around the other text, the text is the same size.

7. Add your job title in another text style (**Title** or **Body**).

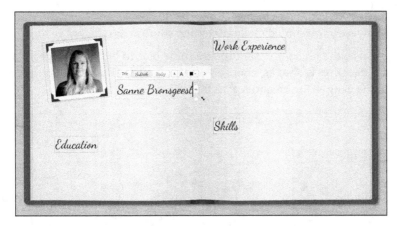

We would like to start our prezumé with our personal message. In the assets of the scrapbook, there is a nice text balloon we can use.

8. Zoom in to the assets, choose the text balloon you want to use, make it bigger, and drag it next to the photo.

9. Then, click on the canvas to add text and in the text box type the message from the paper where you wrote your job, message, and goal. Resize the text to fit it nicely in the box.

10. If you want, you can add a heart from the assets to visually show that this is your real passion.

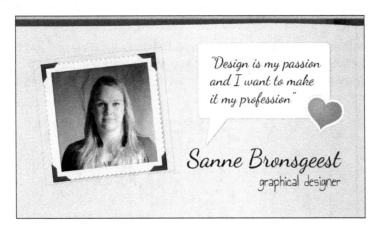

11. Now, add the rest of the text to your prezi. Use the highlighted parts from your résumé.

    For this prezumé, it's important to show our work. So, we'll leave enough space for our **Work Experience**. Here, we want to show our portfolio.

12. Add images of your work to the canvas. If you have less visual work, you could use text; however, you should really try to find some images.

13. We like nice details, so we want to add some pins to lock the images. Navigate to **Insert** | **Symbols & shapes**, choose a style (we used **Photographic**), and drag the pin to the canvas. Resize and rotate the pin.

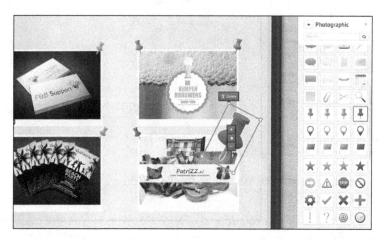

We are almost done with our prezumé.

14. Make a screenshot of your website (or an important project) and add it to your prezi. Navigate to **Insert** | **Symbols & shapes**, select **Simple Dark**, and add the tablet symbol to the canvas. Place the screen of your website in the tablet. Make sure the image is between the tablet and the scrapbook.

15. Add another photo frame (or copy the existing one) and place it just outside the scrapbook. It's nice to use a contact photo if you have one (or just make one). Add another text balloon for your contact details. Use social media symbols from the symbols library.

Our prezumé is full.

16. Now, remove the things that you don't need anymore from your canvas. The easiest way to do this is to hold down the *Shift* key, click and drag a rectangle around the items, and delete everything at once.

17. Let's add a path to our prezi and we're done! We'll start our prezi with our message.

18. Zoom into the text balloon, navigate to **Frames & Arrows | Draw Invisible Frame**, and draw an invisible frame around the text balloon. Rotate the frame a bit to give the frame a different rotation than the text balloon.

19. Add an invisible frame to the path.

20. Zoom out till your photo and your name are visible. Then, draw a new invisible frame around your photo, name, and text balloon. Add this frame to the path.

21. Do the same for your **Education**, **Work Experience**, and **Skills**.

22. The next path steps are: the whole scrapbook, the whole prezi, zoom in to contact photo, zoom in to contact details, and the last step is the complete overview of your prezi. So, our prezumé is finished! It is shown in the following screenshot:

Objective complete – mini debriefing

We used an existing template to create our prezumé in Prezi, and we did a good job of collecting and structuring content before we started our prezi. Therefore, our complete focus was on our prezi and not on choosing what to add to our prezumé. This is more efficient and gives a better result.

We started our prezi with an empty scrapbook and added the text and images. We used a few nice symbols to spice it up and finally, we added a path to create a logical flow. Don't make the path too long, because you want the visitor to reach the end of your prezumé.

Sharing your prezumé

When your prezumé is finished, you are not finished. Your prezumé will not reach your perfect job automatically. You'll have to share it first.

Prepare for lift off

Before you can share your prezi, you have to make it public. Maybe it's already public, but you better check this. If you have a free Public account your prezi will automatically be public and reusable by default. If you have a paid account or an educational Enjoy account, your prezis will be private by default.

If you do not want to make your prezi public, but you still want to share it, you'll also have plenty of options. Just keep reading.

You check whether your prezi is public. Go to `prezi.com`, click on the **Your prezis** tab, find your prezume and click on it. At the bottom-right corner, just under your prezi, you'll find the privacy status (**Public & reusable**, **Public**, **Hidden**, or **Private**). Click on the status if you want to change it. If you're still in the Prezi editor, first save and close your prezi by clicking on the **Exit** button.

A free Public account

With a free Public account, you'll have two options:

▸ **Public & reusable**

▸ **Public**

This is easy because your prezi is automatically public. The default value is **Public & reusable**. Reusable means that everyone can make a copy of your prezi to their account and reuse your content. If you don't want that, uncheck the checkbox **Allow public reuse and help spread ideas**, as shown in the following screenshot:

Enjoy or Pro account

If you have a paid account or an educational account (Enjoy or Pro), you'll have four options:

- ▶ **Public & reusable**
- ▶ **Public**
- ▶ **Hidden**
- ▶ **Private**

The default value is **Hidden**, as shown in the following screenshot:

Use the option **Private** if you don't want anyone to view your prezi unless you invite them. If you keep the option **Hidden**, your prezi will be viewable by link but not searchable on `prezi.com/explore`.

Move the slider to **Public** to make your prezi public or to **Reusable** to make it public and reusable.

If you want to keep your prezumé private, you can still share your prezi to specific people. However, if you want to share it with a large audience, you should set your prezi to public so that other people can share your prezumé too.

Engage thrusters

Ready to share your prezumé?

Go to `prezi.com`, click on the **Your prezis** tab, and find and click your prezumé. Click on the **Share** button under your prezi. You might notice this is the same window where you set your privacy level. So, if you want, you can set both at the same time.

You can share your prezumé in several ways:

 ► Sharing with the world
 ► Sharing with a specific person

▸ Embedding your prezumé on your website

▸ Adding your prezi to your Facebook timeline

Sharing with the world

The following steps will show you how to share your prezi with the world:

1. You can choose from three privacy levels: **Public & reusable**, **Public**, and **Hidden**.

2. Click on the **Copy link** button and paste it into these channels as shown in the following screenshot:

Sharing with a specific person

If you want to have more control over your sharing, you can also share your prezumé with a specific person. You can do that at every level. So, you can keep your prezi private and still share it.

Perform the following steps to share your prezi with a specific person:

1. In the **Add people** box, fill in the e-mail address of the person that you want to share your prezi with.

2. Choose **Viewer** and click on the button **Add**. An e-mail is sent with a link of the prezi. You can add more than one person who can view your prezi and you can also remove them later, as shown in the following screenshot:

If you want the person be able to edit your prezi, you could click on **Editor**, but when you're looking for a job, that won't be the case.

Embedding your prezumé on your website

To reach a large audience, you can embed your prezumé in your website. Perform the following steps:

1. Go to **Your prezis** and click on your prezumé. Click on the **Embed** button under your prezi.

2. If you want, you can change the size of the prezi and you can restrict the visitors to simple back and forward steps. Usually, the default values will do.

3. Click on **Copy code to clipboard** and paste it into the HTML of your website, as shown in the following screenshot. If you have no idea how HTML works, just ask your web designer.

If you are using WordPress, you can paste the code into HTML by clicking on the HTML tab first instead of WYSIWYG.

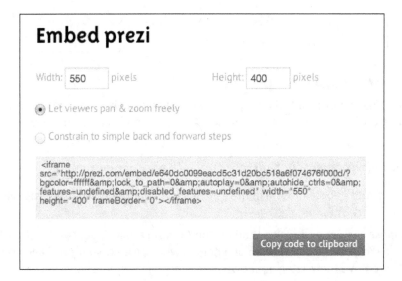

An embedded prezi looks like the following screenshot:

Adding prezi to your Facebook timeline

Facebook is very popular, so it might be a good idea to share your prezi via this channel. It's very easy. Perform the following steps:

1. Go to **Your prezis** and click on your prezumé.

2. Select the URL of the prezi from the address bar of your browser and copy it with the *Ctrl/Command + C* keys.

3. Open your Facebook account, type a message in the new status box, and paste the URL of your prezi with the *Ctrl/Command + V* keys. Facebook will find the picture of your prezi itself and automatically add it after a few seconds.

4. After you post your message, both the URL and the image will be a hyperlink to your prezi, as shown in the following screenshot:

Objective complete – mini debriefing

In this task, you learned how to make your prezi public, how to share it with the world or with a specific person, and how to embed your prezumé in your website.

Now, you're ready to conquer the world!

Mission accomplished

Prezi is great for job hunting. If you create a prezumé, you are one step ahead of other job seekers. Creative people especially benefit from using Prezi because it helps them to show their capabilities.

In this project, we just started building a prezi. We started off by answering three most important questions:

- ▸ What job are you looking for?
- ▸ What message do you want to tell?
- ▸ What's your goal?

Then, we started gathering all the information by writing our résumé and collecting the visual material. Because we don't need all the information in our prezumé, we marked the most important stuff.

The next step was getting creative, but luckily you didn't have to invent everything. We can use predefined templates for your prezumé, and we did just that.

The last step was sharing your prezi with the world or with a specific HT manager or job hunter. Good luck with your new job!

A Hotshot challenge

For this project, you used a predefined template. Now, go ahead and create your own unique prezumé. Use one of the following ideas:

- ▶ Use a timeline to list your education, job experience, and skills in a chronological order.
- ▶ Use one word to put all the information in. The word could be the job title, your name, or the name of the company.
- ▶ Use a really cool image that expresses your passion.

Project 3

I Want to Use Prezi for My Lessons

Prezi is a nice tool to create learning materials, such as lesson content, especially because you can give people both an overview and the details. You can also switch easily between topics if necessary. In this way, a hierarchy of information can easily be explained.

Mission briefing

In this project, we'll create a lesson in Prezi. We don't just start in Prezi, we first think about the lesson that should be learned and the goals that should be reached. Of course, we'll also create the content of the lesson. It's important to think both about the overview and the details. What are the main topics? How many topics do you need? What does the overview look like? How do you explain specific details? How can you switch between topics?

We not only think about the content, we also create the content in Prezi. After the lesson is over, maybe you would want to test your students or the students can test themselves. Maybe you'll give them an assignment to work on? You can put all this information in the prezi as well. So, every student has a complete overview of the lesson at all times.

We can even go a step further and share the prezi with our students so that they can add their content and remarks. Alternatively, the students can use the new collaboration tools to work together and create their own project in Prezi.

The lesson we'll create in this project is a lesson about bees. We use information found at `simple.wikipedia.org/wiki/Bee` and `en.wikipedia.org/wiki/Bee`. We can make this lesson as complicated and large as we want. However, for this project, we'll try to keep it simple, as shown in the following screenshot:

Why is it awesome?

Prezi is great for education. Teachers can use Prezi to present lessons and they can share their prezis with other teachers. On the Explore page of `prezi.com`, you can search through millions of prezis.

Students can use Prezi to present their projects, to brainstorm new projects, and also to mind map. Also, young children can use Prezi to create projects for school. It's amazing how fast young children learn and usually they start using Prezi right away. In our experience, they love it! They do not (yet) think in slides and zooming in and out: nonlinear thinking comes naturally to them.

Students can even work together in Prezi with the new collaboration tools. They don't need to sit together or work at the same time. They only need a Prezi account and they can work together in the same prezi.

It's amazing how enthusiastic students can become about Prezi!

Your Hotshot objectives

The major tasks to complete this project are:

- ▸ Identifying learning content
- ▸ Creating an overview
- ▸ Creating the content
- ▸ Determining the look and feel
- ▸ Switching between topics

Mission checklist

There are no special requirements for this project.

Identifying learning content

Before we start creating our lesson in Prezi, we have to determine what lesson should be learned. We have to define one or more goals first.

Prepare for lift off

Our focus group is children between the age of 8-12 years. We want to teach them the following:

- ▸ What are bees?
- ▸ The different kinds of bees
- ▸ The body of the bee
- ▸ What is pollination?
- ▸ Evolution of the bee
- ▸ Do all bees live together?
- ▸ Kinds of bees in a colony
- ▸ The importance of bees

We can find all the information about bees on Wikipedia and, of course, you could also use other reference sources. These goals form our main topics.

Engage thrusters

Let's first create a structure for our lesson in Prezi. You can use paper or post-its as well, but by working directly in Prezi, it's easier to move content and show a hierarchy.

Open a new prezi, choose the **Blank** template, and delete all the objects on the canvas. Make sure your canvas is completely empty. Then, type (or copy) the goals of your lesson on to the canvas. Please don't make a list, put the information organically on the canvas as shown in the following screenshot:

```
            What bees are?

                          Evolution of the bee
Different kind of bees

                              Do all bees live together?
      The bee body

                     Kinds of bees in a colony
  What is pollination?

            The importance of bees
```

We could keep all the eight goals as main topics, but we can also create more structured content. Let's keep five main topics in this lesson. These are as follows:

- ▸ What are bees?
- ▸ What is pollination?
- ▸ Evolution of the bee
- ▸ Do all bees live together?
- ▸ The importance of bees

The remaining topics will become subtopics. The topics *Different kind of bees* and *The bee body* are subtopics of *What bees are?* and the topic *Kinds of bees in a colony* will become a subtopic of *Do all bees live together?* Let's first add a title to our prezi.

Click on the canvas and type The world of bees. Choose the text style **Title** for it and make it big.

Double-click on the five main topics on the canvas one by one and choose the text style **Subtitle** for them. Make the subtopics a bit bigger. Move the subtopics closer to the main topic where they belong.

Finally, open the **Theme Wizard** by navigating to **Themes | Customize Current Theme** and change the colors of your prezi. We chose the colors blue and green as shown in the following screenshot:

The world of bees

What bees are?

Different kind of bees

The bee body

Evolution of the bee

Do all bees live together?

Kinds of bees in a colony

What is pollination?

The importance of bees

Objective complete – mini debriefing

We started this project by defining what lesson should be learned and by whom. We haven't created all the content yet. We defined the goals of our lesson and made a rough structure of the lesson in Prezi. These steps might seem simple, but they are important. If you have these steps right, the rest is normally straightforward.

Creating an overview

Overview is the key to a good prezi. This is especially true for educational prezis.

Prepare for lift off

We already started creating an overview in the previous task. In this task, we'll add frames to it and finish the complete structure of the overview. In the next task, we'll only have to fill it in.

We'll use Wikipedia as the source for our structure. We won't insert images or videos yet, just text.

Engage thrusters

Draw five circle frames around the five main topics. Maybe you have to move the frames a bit so that they don't overlap.

The frames don't have to be of the same size. If you think certain topics are more important, you can draw a larger frame around it. Don't draw a bigger frame because you think the information won't fit in the frame. You can always scale the content to make it fit. Change the sentences of the main topics into single words as much as you can.

For example, we can change *What bees are?* to just *Bees* and *Evolution of the bee* to just **Evolution**. Also, draw frames around the subtopics as shown in the following screenshot:

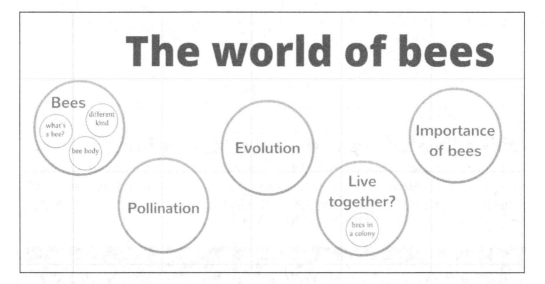

Go through the content, find topics and further subtopics, and put them in your prezi. Do not fill your prezi completely; remember that you are building the structure of your prezi now. Our prezi now looks like the following screenshot:

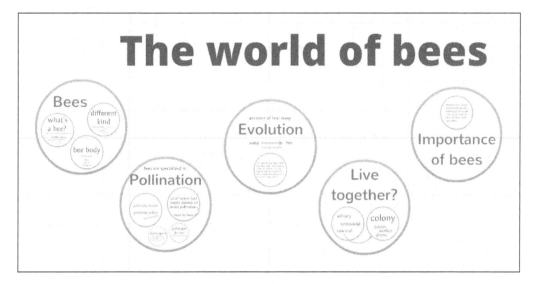

Objective complete – mini debriefing

In this task, we created the complete structure of our prezi. We worked from the main topics to the sub-ordinate topics. Since we have not used any images till now, we have been able to keep our focus on the structure and content. Now, let's fill our prezi.

Classified intel

Following this step-by-step procedure saves you from repeating it over and over again. While working on your structure, you can still easily move around the objects and make the objects larger and smaller and therefore more or less important, respectively.

When you finish your structure completely, before adding images, videos, and design elements, you are most flexible.

Creating the content

This task requires less thinking and more doing since we have to fill in the details of our prezi.

Prepare for lift off

Use content you are allowed to use. If you use images from the Internet, make sure they are not protected by copyright licenses. Usually, you can use images from Wikipedia pages, but take careful note of the licensing conditions for every image.

Engage thrusters

We won't describe all the content we added to our prezi. We'll only show you some highlights. We'll make use of post-its to highlight important subjects of the prezi. It's a good way to focus on certain content. Perform the following steps to create the content:

1. Select **Sketched** by navigating to **Insert | Symbols & shapes...**.

2. Drag the post-it to the canvas and resize it.

3. Place the text on the post-it. If it's behind the post-it, use the right mouse button to choose **Bring to Front**.

4. If you can replace text with images, please do so. Sometimes, it's necessary to add text to images. For instance, if you look at the four different pictures of the four groups of bees, you can't tell what kind of bees they are; then it's necessary to add text.

When you want to use pictures from Wikipedia pages, make sure you download a high resolution photo. This works as follows:

1. Select a picture on a Wikipedia page.

2. Now, you can look at a preview of the picture that you could download. Under the picture, you'll find various formats of picture sizes. Choose the highest resolution (or around 1000 pixels).

3. When the pictures appear onscreen, right-click on the picture and choose **Save this image as**.

4. Save the picture and add it to your prezi by navigating to **Insert | Image**, as shown in the next screenshot:

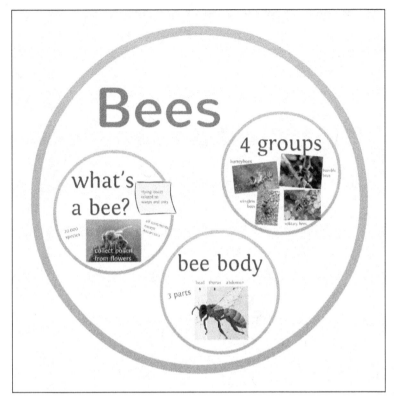

Subtopic: Bees

In the next screenshot, you'll see another two post-its. However, most importantly, you'll see the big *dislike* thumb. This symbol works well in two ways:

▸ The thumbs-down symbol means negativity or disapproval

▸ The thumbs-down image is also directly linked to the subject of the decline in pollinators

Subtopic: Pollination

In the next screenshot, which shows the subtopic **Evolution**, you can see that we used an arrow to symbolize the *from* and *to* states. Of course, we also added pictures to show what a wasp and a bee look like. There's not much information in this frame, but it's enough to explain the core of what we want to say.

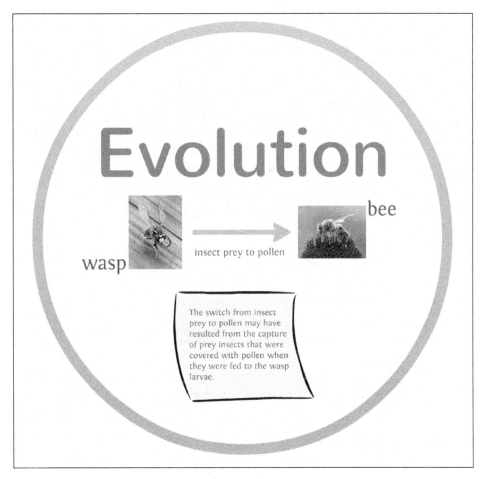

Subtopic: Evolution

The next screenshot, which shows the subtopic **Importance of bees**, is even simpler. The importance is symbolized by the exclamation mark, and because it's so important, there is even less content than the other frames to make the information stand out. We also added the sources of the content to the prezi and a post-it with an assignment for the students.

Subtopic: Importance of bees

Take a look at the prezi *World of bees* at www.prezihotshot.com.

Objective complete – mini debriefing

We did a good job in this task and filled our whole prezi with nice content. The prezi now looks like following:

You could stop here, but you can also go a step further and make your prezi look even better—like a real designer!

Determining the look and feel

You might think a prezi doesn't need a great look and feel, but learning is much more fun if it looks great. Also, well designed information tends to be understood and remembered more easily.

Prepare for lift off

Until now, we used circle-shaped frames for our structure in Prezi. Although it looks good, the circle shape is not related to bees. We all know a honeycomb is made up of hexagons. Wouldn't it be a good idea if we could replace our circles with hexagons? We are lucky. Prezi just released a new template with hexagons in it. Yay!

Leave the prezi about bees that you already have open in your browser, go to the **Your prezis** tab, and click on **New prezi**. A new tab is opened with the new prezi.

Engage thrusters

When you open the new prezi, first you have to choose a template. Choose the template **Brainstorm with Cubes** and click on **Use template**. This template contains hexagons, as shown in the following screenshot. At www.prezihotshot.com, you'll find the link to this template. We only need one hexagon for our prezi.

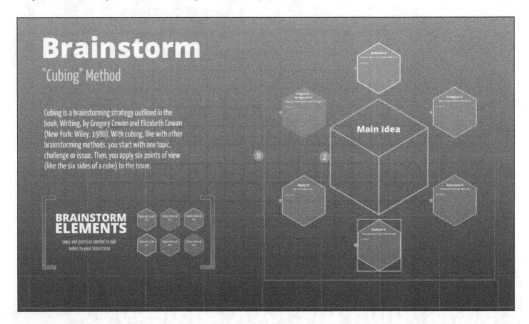

Select one of the hexagons (just click on it) and use the *Ctrl/Cmd + C* keys to copy it. Click on the tab with the prezi **World of bees** and paste the hexagon on the canvas. Make sure you place the hexagon on an empty spot of the prezi. If necessary, zoom out to create space.

Now, let's create a sort of honeycomb. Select the hexagon (if it's not already selected) and use the *Ctrl/Cmd + D* keys to duplicate it several times. Make a image similar to what is shown in the next screenshot. If necessary, you can add more hexagons later.

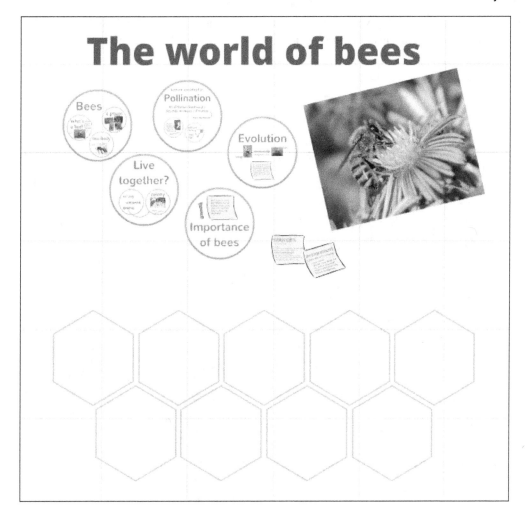

Next, we'll use one of the pictures as a background image.

Copy and paste one of the pictures from your prezi (or insert another one) and make it really big. Select the picture, click the right mouse button, and select **Send to Back** to put it behind the honeycomb, as shown in the following screenshot:

Now, fill the honeycomb with the content of your prezi. Maybe add or remove a few hexagons. Start with adding the title `World of bees` to the new prezi. Copy the title **World of bees** to the large image just above the hexagons. For this background, we have to change the color of the title.

Click on the title, select **Edit Text**, select the whole text by clicking-and-dragging, and select the white color.

As you can see in the next screenshot, we also rearranged the hexagons a bit.

Now, let's move all the content to the hexagons. It's ok if a few hexagons are empty. However, first we'll make sure the content will be on top of the large image and the hexagons.

Hold down the *Shift* key and click on all the hexagons (you can also click-and-drag while holding down the *Shift* key). Then, right-click and select **Send to Back**. All hexagons will now disappear behind the large image.

Zoom out, deselect all hexagons, right-click on the large image, and select **Send to Back** again. The large image moves behind the hexagons and the hexagons will be visible again.

Now, when you move a content frame to the large image, you know for sure that the content will be on top of the hexagons. This is important so you have the ability to select all the different parts. Also this is better for presenting because now you can just click on a part of the content and Prezi zooms into it.

You are ready to move the content to the hexagons. Click-and-drag the first frame with content **Bees over a hexagon**. Because the frames group the content, you only have to drag the frame, the content will remain in the frame. This is shown in the following screenshot:

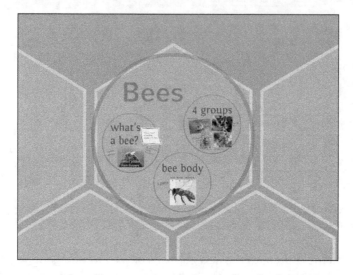

Click on the frame and choose **Remove frame** from the **Frame** menu options. This removes the frame without affecting the content. Let's also change the style a bit.

Navigate to **Themes | Customize Current Theme** and select white for the subtitle and orange for the circle frames. Navigate to **Insert | Symbol & shapes... | Photographic** and drag the yellow post-it to the canvas. Put it in place of the sketchy post-it. The new look is as follows:

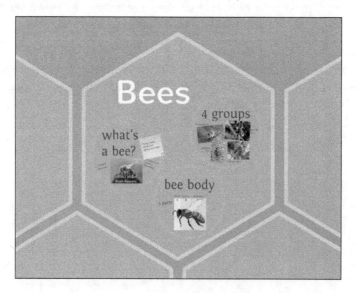

In the same way, you can move the rest of the content to the hexagons and change the post-its. We've got a whole new look now, as shown in the following screenshot:

The final step that you have to take is creating your path. We'll do that in the next task.

Objective complete – mini debriefing

We changed our prezi to another design in this task. We used a very large image as the base for the new prezi. We also used a hexagon to build a honeycomb in our prezi and we put the content in it.

Finally, we also changed the look and a feel by choosing other colors for text and frames, and we replaced the sketchy post-its with more photographic post-its.

Classified intel

We put the large image on the canvas and positioned the hexagons on the images. For a whole different effect, try putting the image in the prezi as a 3D background. This can be done by performing the following steps:

1. Delete the large image from the canvas.

2. Select **Customize Current Theme** under **Themes**.

3. Click on the **Upload** button under **3D Background** and select the image. Then, click on **Done**. The final result is shown in the following screenshot:

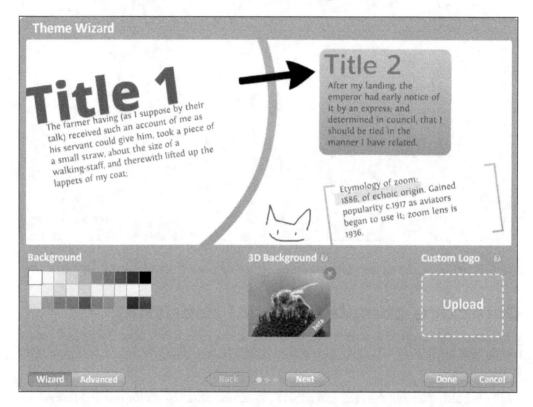

We repositioned the content, but we don't have full control over the position of the content due to the **3D Background**. Zoom in and out a bit and watch the effect. You'll see the background is moving differently than the content. This depends on the zoom status.

At www.prezihotshot.com, you'll find our prezi with the large image of the bee as the 3D background. Play with it and watch the effect.

Switching between topics

For educational prezis, it's important to be able to switch easily between topics. Not only for the teacher so that he or she can go back or forward if a student asks a question, but also for the students when they go through the prezi by themselves.

Of course, it is important to create a good structure and a good overview, but it is also important to know how to use Prezi well. For instance, you should know where to click to navigate easily through the prezi.

Engage thrusters

Let's create the path for our prezi.

Creating the path

For an educational prezi, it's a good idea to start with the overview of your content. It can be created by performing the following steps:

1. Click on **Frames & Arrows**, select **Draw Invisible Frame**, and draw a rectangle around the honeycomb that contains our content.

2. Click on the pencil at the left side of the screen (**Edit path**) and click on the invisible frame you just drew. This will add it to the path of our prezi as shown in the following screenshot:

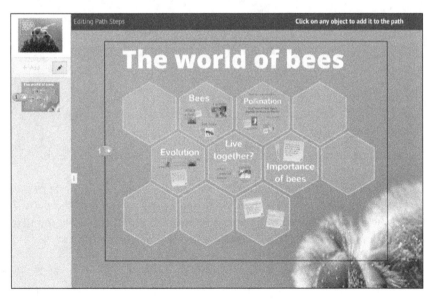

Now, we'll create the rest of the path.

3. Make sure you are still in the **Editing Path steps** mode or click on the pencil to edit the path again. Click on the hexagon of the first subject, then zoom in and add the other frames to the path. Also, add the post-its to the path. Draw an invisible frame around the image of the bee body and the words **head, thorax**, and **abdomen**, and add this frame to the path.

4. After adding the content of the first subject to the path, add the large invisible frame again to the path. After showing each subject, we'll show the overview of our content.

   Continue with the next subject and add the overview. Repeat this for all the subjects, as shown in the following screenshot:

5. Zoom out to make the large image visible and draw another invisible frame on it. Make this frame a bit smaller than the image itself and add it to the path. We make this frame a bit smaller than the image to make sure that the background is invisible when we present our prezi, as shown in the following screenshot:

Navigating through the prezi

It's time to present our prezi!

Click on the **Present** button and navigate through your prezi using the arrows at the bottom. This way, you can navigate by following the path you created yourself. If one of your students asks a question, you might want to go back to the overview or straight to another subject. Perhaps you want to switch topics frequently.

When you are somewhere deep inside a subject and you have to show the overview of your content, you can't click on the small house at the right side of the screen (which you usually should do), because you would zoom out too much. Instead, you would click on the canvas somewhere. Because you are inside a subject, you will click on the hexagon of that subject and Prezi will zoom out to the whole hexagon. If you click outside a hexagon once more, you will get the overview.

This way, you can easily navigate through your prezi without using the path, just by clicking on the hexagons, frames, and (if you want) images on the canvas. Make sure you test it yourself before doing it in front of your class.

If you're lost in your own prezi, you can always use the down arrow of your keyboard a few times to find the overview again. You could also click the small house button at the right side of the screen to show the whole prezi, but then you'll spoil the nice surprise that was meant for the end of your lesson.

Objective complete – mini debriefing

This task taught us how to create a path in our prezi that was created for educational purposes. It's important to show the overview of the content between each subject. Make sure you provide a good overview and a clear structure.

Another important thing is that you should be able to navigate through your prezi without the path. You learned how to do that in this task. You use the objects of the canvas to zoom in to them and the canvas itself to zoom out. Also, there's always the small house button at the right side of the screen to show the whole prezi.

Mission accomplished

In this project, we created an educational prezi. We found the content on Wikipedia. First, we defined learning content and our goals. We translated these goals to main topics and subtopics of our lesson.

In our Prezi, we created the structure of our lesson. Gradually, we added content. First we added the main content, and then we added the details. After the complete structure of our lesson was (in text) ready, we added pictures to the prezi.

Our final prezi looked like the following:

The last part of this project was to spice up our prezi a bit more by using one large image as a background of our prezi. In this way, we made our prezi more designed in style. A more designed, final prezi would look like the following:

A Hotshot challenge

Share your prezi with your students by using the collaboration features of Prezi. Let your students add their own content to your prezi. Don't forget to make a copy of it before you share your prezi with your students. If someone makes a mistake and deletes all the content, you can always go back to your saved copy.

Students can also use the collaboration features to work on the same prezi together, independent of the time and location. You'll find all the information about Prezi collaboration features at `prezi.com/collaborate`.

Also, an official collaboration tutorial is available at `prezi.com/pev6l3yr6yor/official-collaboration-tutorial`.

Project 4

Designing a Serious Corporate Presentation

Corporate presentations are often boring. They consist of too much text, too many bullet points, ugly images, and unreadable graphs. The presenter is reading out loud what's on the slides and that's it. Boring.

We can't enhance the presenter's skills in this project, but we can help you build a better corporate presentation. This will also help you to become a better presenter.

Mission briefing

The average business presentation looks like a slide deck full of bullets. This happens because people use their presentation as a tool to think of the content of their presentation. They try to create their story and to design their presentation at the same time. It just doesn't work.

No one can do these things at the same time. Not even the best presentation designers! First, you should think of the story you want to tell, and then start designing your presentation. We can't turn you in a designer at once, but we can help you by showing a better workflow and teaching you simple design principles that you can apply to your presentation to get better results.

We developed a seven-step workflow especially to create presentations in Prezi. This will definitely improve your presentations. In this project, you will learn how to use our method to design and build your corporate presentation. We used the Seats2meet.com concept for our project.

The unexpected relevance when meeting people at a Seats2meet.com location is our extreme, co-created added value: serendipity.

The Seats2meet.com concept facilitates a dynamic environment for people to work together, meet each other, and to share knowledge. It is an environment where people can use their knowledge, expertise, and enthusiasm to add value for the greater good.

Seats2meet.com was founded in 2007, opening its first physical location in Utrecht, The Netherlands. Seats2meet.com International is a part of CDEF Holding, which was founded in 2003 by Mariëlle Sijgers and Ronald van den Hoff.

Why is it awesome?

The most important things that people think about when designing and building their business presentation in Prezi are as follows:

- How do I incorporate our style guide?
- Can I create a handout?
- How can I make our logo visible at all times?

All three could be important but actually they are not. The first thing that's important is reaching your goal and the second is telling a story.

You can have a fantastic presentation without your corporate colors and fonts, without having handouts, and without a logo in your presentation. However, you can't have a great presentation without a clear goal and a good story.

In this project, we will learn our unique seven-step method to define a clear strategy, develop your content, think of a good concept, choosing colors, and fonts, and finally create your corporate prezi.

The steps of our method are as follows:

1. Strategy
2. Brainstorming
3. Title and keywords
4. Concept
5. Story
6. Storyboard
7. Design

Your Hotshot objectives

The major tasks to complete this project are as follows:

► Defining your strategy
► Brainstorming the content
► Defining the title and keywords
► Thinking of a good concept
► What's the story you want to tell?
► Creating your storyboard
► Defining colors, fonts, and other design issues
► Creating the presentation in Prezi

Mission checklist

In this project, we'll start on paper. You will need at least seven pages, one for every step. Number the pages one to seven. You'll probably need some more, so grab some more and keep it within reach. It's very important to write everything down. Don't think that it's enough to do it in your head. Writing it down makes it definitive and you can think about it more thoroughly. You can also download and print our blank workbook at www.prezihotshot.com.

 Download our filled example workbook, which we refer to during the course of this project, at www.prezihotshot.com.

The focus of this project is a business presentation. However, you can use our method for every presentation.

Defining your strategy

The very first step is defining the strategy of your presentation. It consists of three parts:

- ▸ Goal
- ▸ Message
- ▸ Audience

Prepare for lift off

Take a piece of paper with the number one on it. Draw three boxes on it and write GOAL, MESSAGE, and AUDIENCE above the three boxes.

Engage thrusters

This step is the most important step of the whole method. Define it well and look regularly back at it.

What's your goal?

Define your goal in one sentence. Think of what you want to achieve with the presentation and write it down. What do you want the audience to do after your presentation? Should they call you? Should they send you an e-mail? Should they immediately buy your new product? Do you want them to ask for more information? Think of one (yes one) specific goal and write it down in one sentence in the GOAL box.

Be as specific as possible and avoid vague language. Don't write down the mission statement or vision of your company, because that's not what you want to reach with your presentation. Most of the time, you want to sell something. A business presentation is mostly about sales.

By defining one goal, you are not only focused, it's also easier to measure the success of your presentation. It's better to go for one small goal then try to reach for the impossible.

What's your message?

While defining the message, you should think about what you want your audience to remember after your presentation. A good practice is to think about what you want your audience to say about your presentation when they get home.

What I mean is, after someone attended your presentation, what do they say at home about your presentation? What do you want them to say at home? Write that sentence in the MESSAGE box.

Who's your audience?

Describe who your audience is. Think of gender, age, education, number of people, language, and nationality. What do they already know about your company, about you, about your products, and services? Try to describe as much as possible and write it down in the AUDIENCE box.

If you'll use the presentation not in front of a live audience, but on a website or for an exhibition for instance, you should write that down as well. Standalone prezis (that's how we call them) might need more text or a voice-over, since there's no presenter to tell the story. Our finished strategy now looks like the following screenshot:

Workbook: **presentation Seats2meet.com concept**

I. Strategy

Goal
What do you want to achieve with this presentation?

> I want the attendees to register for our virtual of physical "Introduction to the Concept" seminar, in which we will elaborate on the concept and where they can meet other entrepreneurs.

Message
Think about what you want your audience to tell about your presentation when they get home.

> I am a fan of the Seats2meet.com concept and its growing (international) network of interesting people. I would like to start my own S2M location in my region.
> I will register for that seminar right away!

Audience
Describe your audience.

> New (to be) international S2M entrepreneurs.

Objective complete – mini debriefing

We took the first step of our journey to create better business presentations. We defined our goal, described the message, and defined our audience.

Classified intel

Remember this is the most important step of the process. It's a good idea to look back at your strategy after every step that you complete.

Brainstorming the content

The next step of our method is brainstorming. You can do this in different kinds of ways. You can use paper for it, sticky notes (post-its), and even Prezi. If you want to use Prezi for your brainstorm, just have a look at the first project of this book. That's where we explained it.

Prepare for lift off

The small yellow sticky notes work very well for brainstorming. Make sure you have enough to write down the word explosion that will grow in your brain in a few moments.

Engage thrusters

The art of a good brainstorm is not to think too much. That might seem a contradiction, but the idea is that we want to stimulate our creative right brain. Structured thinking is more a left-brain activity.

Read your goal, message, and audience once more and write down every word that pops up in your mind on a sticky note. Use one word per sticky note. If a word seems irrelevant, don't think about it, just write it down. Brainstorming is about associations and thinking of new ideas. If you don't write down every word, you might skip the best idea.

Continue brainstorming for at least half an hour. When you're satisfied, you're finished. If you're not satisfied yet, take a break for half an hour and continue brainstorming for another half hour.

In the beginning, you will be focused only on your company and products. However, try to forget that and make new associations. Try to make associations from associations. It's okay if a word has nothing to do with your business. It's even better, because that means you are being creative.

One of the words might form your design concept or the metaphor for your presentation. Stick all the post-its on the piece of paper with number two on it. If there's not enough room, just use multiple pieces of paper. The following image will be our result:

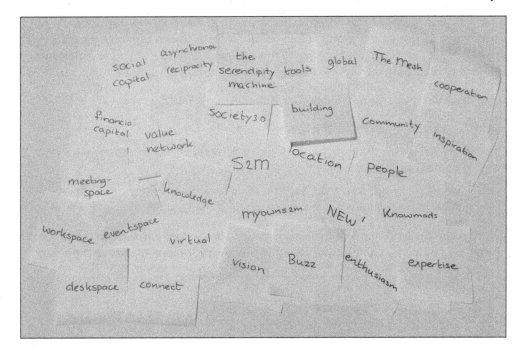

Objective complete – mini debriefing

In the second step, we brainstormed the content of our presentation. We used sticky notes for this and wrote down one word on every sticky note.

Defining the title and keywords

In this step, we will define the title for our presentation and the three most important keywords. Later, these three keywords will become the main subjects of our presentation.

Prepare for lift off

We'll use our brainstorm from the second step to define the most important keywords. Grab paper number three. Draw one large box and write Title above it, draw three smaller boxes next to each other, and write the word Keywords above it.

Engage thrusters

First of all, define a good title for your presentation. Maybe you won't use the title inside the prezi, but at least you will use as the title for your presentation to recognize your prezi and to be able to talk about this specific presentation. The title shouldn't be too long. One sentence will do.

The next thing you'll have to do is to decide on the most important words from your brainstorm. Pick exactly three words from your brainstorm. In order to force yourself to just pick three keywords, you really have to think through what are the most important words in your brainstorm. It helps you a lot to define what's really important.

You can mark the keywords in the following different ways:

- ▶ Use a highlighter to mark the keywords
- ▶ Write the keywords on sticky notes with a different color and put them back on your brainstorm paper
- ▶ Take the sticky notes with the keywords and stick them on the boxes of paper number three

If you mark the keywords on your brainstorm paper, also write them down in the boxes of the piece of paper for step number three. The following is our result of the third step:

---

3. Title and keywords

Title

Start your own Seats2meet.com location!

Choose 3 keywords

vision	community	myowns2m

Objective complete – mini debriefing

In this step, we defined the title of our prezi and we found the three most important words in our brainstorm. These words are the keywords of our information and will be the three subjects of our presentation.

Thinking of a good concept

Step four in our process of creating our business presentation is thinking of a good concept. Creativity is necessary here! However, being creative is not that hard as you might think. We have lots of examples and good ideas for you to get creative.

Engage thrusters

The concept for our presentation is the creative idea. This could be a photograph, an illustration, one word, or the logo of the company itself for example. Decide what you want the overview of your prezi to look like. That's your basic concept. Later, you can fill in the details.

Try to think in images. The following ideas can help you:

- ▸ Go to Google Images and search with one of your keywords. Scroll through the images and get inspiration.

- ▸ Go to a stock photo site, such as www.istockphoto.com and do the same. You might see entirely different images than in the previous search.

- ▸ Do the same with www.pinterest.com.

 You can't just use the images you found via Google Images or on www.istockphoto.com. You have to ask permission to use them or pay for them. Please don't violate copyright laws.

Describe or draw the creative ideas on paper number four. Remember that usually your creative concept is the overview of your prezi.

 If you find it very hard to think of a creative concept, first write your story in the next step, and then return to this step.

Examples of creative concepts

Five examples of creative concepts are given here. The images show the overview of the prezis. It gives you a good idea of the possibilities and (hopefully) inspiration for your prezi. Of course, you can find these examples on www.prezihotshot.com.

The first example shows the use of a logo for the creative concept. It's a prezi about MASTERPEACE, an international grassroots movement that inspires everyone around the world to use his or her talent and energy to build peace and togetherness. All the information is placed inside the logo.

The second example shows a metaphor. In this prezi, Maria Andersen explains Twitter and she uses a tree (with birds and leaves) as a visual metaphor for Twitter. You probably know the logo of Twitter is a bird.

In the third example, a clock is used to explain 60 apps in 60 minutes.

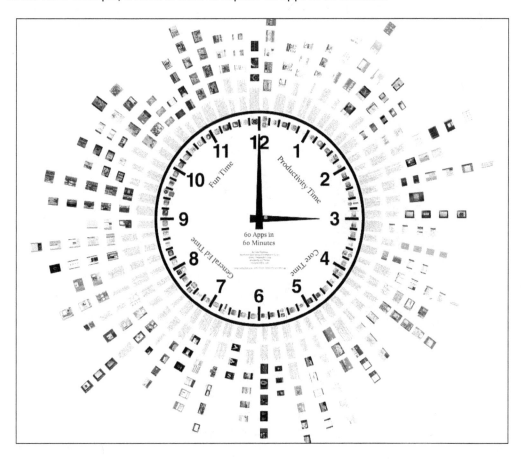

The fourth example shows all the information in one word. This word is the subject of the presentation. It's the TED talk of Ron Gutman, "The Untapped Powers of the Smile." During the presentation, you'll fly through lots of circles and the complete overview is revealed only at the end.

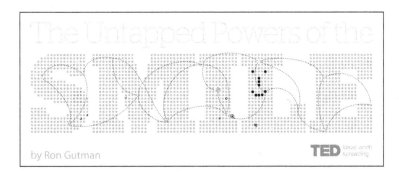

The fifth example is a very nice creative concept from Marcos Xalabarder of `Presentaciones.biz`. He's the runner-up of the TED-Prezi contest, Ideas Matter. His prezi is dedicated to Sarah Kay's TED talk "If I should have a daughter..." and is an amazing story about spoken poetry. It's a must see!

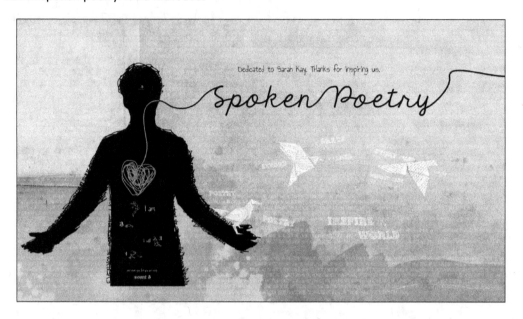

In our creative concept for this project, the logo of the company should play an important role. The presentation is about starting new locations, so we will be using an office building as the image for our overview. We can put the story inside the building. We will start with the logo, *go through* the building, and end our presentation with the image of the whole building. Maybe this seems a simple concept, but most of the time the most simple concepts are the best concepts.

The following is the description of the creative concept for this project:

> *The logo of Seats2meet.com should play an important role in the design of the presentation. It's about starting new Seats2meet.com locations, so the idea is to use an office building as the creative concept.*

> *This office building has the Seats2meet.com logo on it and the windows of the building can contain the information of the presentation.*

> *This was our thinking thread:*

> *Seats2meet.com – logo – S2M – entrepreneur – new location – office – office building*

The following is the image used in the creative concept:

Objective complete – mini debriefing

Step four in our process is the most creative step. Don't think you are not creative. Help your creativity by searching for images on Google Images or stock photo sites. You can get lots of inspiration out of this.

We used one image for our creative concept. This will be the overview of our prezi. Our story will be told inside that image. The logo of the company will also play an important role in our prezi.

Classified intel

It's also a good idea to have a look at other presentations. Go to `prezi.com/explore/` and find out how other people use their creativity in their prezis.

What's the story you want to tell?

The next step in our working process is writing down the story we want to tell. This is the story you will be telling on stage. You don't have to write down the exact words of the story. A short version will be sufficient.

If the presentation won't be told on stage, for instance if your prezi will be used embedded in a website, you can write down the story the viewer should read, look at, and/or hear.

Prepare for lift off

Just grab a pen or pencil and start writing on page number five.

Engage thrusters

Write down your story in simple sentences. Don't try to make it more beautiful and please don't use difficult words. Try to write down your story as simple as possible.

I divided the story of Seats2meet.com in the following five parts:

- ▸ An introduction
- ▸ Vision of Seats2meet.com
- ▸ The community
- ▸ My own s2m
- ▸ Call to action

The following are the last two parts of the story for this project:

(myowns2m)

The Seats2meet.com experience consists of the following:

- ▸ Meetingspace
- ▸ Workspace
- ▸ Deskspace (coming soon)
- ▸ Eventspace (new)

In the business model of Seats2meet.com, we do not only work with financial capital. Social capital is a very important part of the concept. Financial and Social Capital is a beneficial combination.

(call to action)

It's very easy to start your own Seats2meet.com location right now. Just follow our wizard. However, maybe it's a good idea to first register for our seminar and meet other Seats2meet.com entrepreneurs. We love to help you with the starting of your own Seats2meet.com location.

Objective complete – mini debriefing

In step five of our process, we wrote down our story. This is the story we want to tell on the stage. We divided our story into five parts, because that helps up to keep an overview. Also, it's easier to write five small stories than one very large story.

Creating your storyboard

In the last step, you wrote down your story. Now, you are going to transform this story to something visual—a storyboard.

Prepare for lift off

A lot of people are afraid to draw. They say they can't draw. Well, most kids can draw, so most people should be able to draw as well. You don't have to be an artist and we won't hang your storyboard in an art gallery. The storyboard you are creating is just for you. Just for you to create better presentations. Of course, we'll give you the best tips and you'll see that you can create a storyboard as well. So let's move on!

Engage thrusters

This task consists of two parts. First we are going to divide the story into views, and then we are going to draw our storyboard.

Dividing your story into views

The first step in creating our storyboard is to divide the written story into views. Every time the screen changes, there is a different view. You can compare a view to a slide. Actually, we don't like the word *slide*, because that might put you in a PowerPoint mode and that's not what we want right now.

Print your written story and start dividing your story into views. Every time you think something else should be on screen, draw a line next to the sentences to combine them and put a number next to the line.

Take a look at the next image to understand this better:

6. The serendipity machine explains the business model of Seats2meet.com. We
    created a business model that provides a value creation platform for
    knowmads, free agents, or independent professionals as well as corporate
    nomads to unleash their creative powers.
    Find out more about this book on www.serendipitymachine.com.

    Our core values are:

7. Value network
    Collaborating with Seats2meet.com means you will become part of an
    extensive global value network.

8. Social capital
    Social Capital can add value to your location at a variety of ways: not only does
    it provide an enormous amount of reliable Buzz, it also leads to tremendous
    cost reduction.

9. Asynchronous reciprocity
    When you give something you are obligating the receiver of the gift to re-pay
    his or her gift-debt. However, the reciprocity is asynchronous, meaning that
    when and how the repayment takes place is left to the will and capabilities of
    the receiver.

You don't have to visualize everything. The things you will show in your presentation should add value to the story you are telling on stage. Not the other way around! If it's not adding any value, just leave it out. You and what you tell on stage is more important than your presentation.

Drawing your storyboard

Take page number six, put the largest side of the paper at the bottom (landscape), and draw nine rectangles on it. Look at the next image to see how this will look like. You can also download our storyboard example from www.prezihotshot.com as a PDF file so that you can print it.

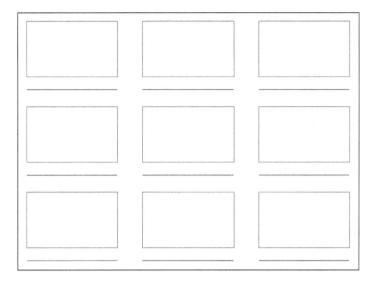

Give every view a number. Also, give the page a number because you might need multiple pages for your storyboard. Then, start drawing your storyboard.

Here are some tips that might help you:

- ▶ Make your drawings as simple as possible.
- ▶ It's ok to use words in your storyboard.
- ▶ Don't try to draw every detail. It's ok to draw a logo as a circle or square.
- ▶ Use symbols to visualize whether you are zooming in (magnifier with plus sign), zooming out (magnifier with minus sign), making a vertical transition (arrow up or down), making a horizontal transition (arrow right or left), or using fade-in animation (plus sign). Put these symbols between the views.
- ▶ If you need to explain something, write it under the rectangle in just a few words.
- ▶ Have some fun while creating your drawings.

Take a look at our storyboard. This is the first page of our storyboard:

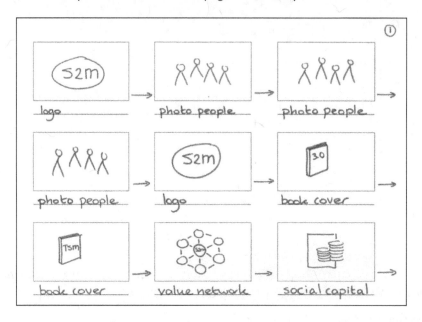

Here is our second page of the storyboard:

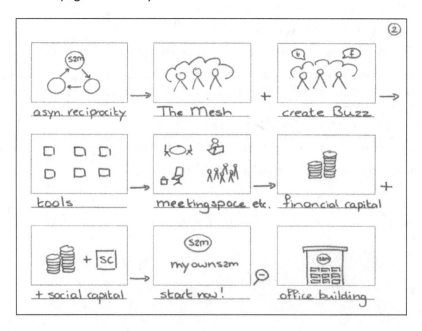

Objective complete – mini debriefing

We have already come really far in our process. In this step, we created the storyboard for our presentation. It's a visual representation of the story we are going to tell on the stage. It's important that you don't visualize every sentence. Remember the things you show in your presentation should be of added value.

Defining colors, fonts, and other design issues

The last step in our seven-step workflow is defining all the design issues for our presentation.

Prepare for lift off

Find out if there's a corporate brand. Think about logo, colors, and fonts. Maybe a style guide is available.

Engage thrusters

If there's a corporate style guide available, find out whether you have to use it and how strict this is. Depending on the type of presentation, you might be allowed not to follow the style guide strictly.

This is especially important for fonts. You can't implement fonts in Prezi yourself. If you can't use the fonts available on Prezi, you have to ask `Prezi.com` to develop a corporate template. This is not free.

The company we are developing our prezi for has a style guide. You can see a screenshot of a page from this guide in the next screenshot and you can download the colored version of the workbook from www.prezihotshot.com.

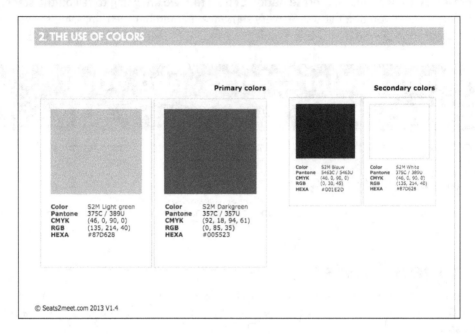

The basic font used for Seats2meet.com is Tahoma. We don't have this font available in Prezi. So, we searched for a font in Prezi that fits best. Our choice is **PT Sans** for body text and **Open Sans Bold** for the title text. We only need two fonts.

The basic color used on the website of Seats2meet.com is **#062C33**. This is a very dark blue. In www.colorpicker.com, we translated this color to RGB value so that we can use it in Prezi. The RGB value is **6**, **44**, **51** as shown in the next screenshot. The style guide mentions other colors too. However, we don't use a lot of text in our prezi and one dark color is enough for our presentation.

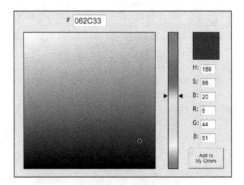

We got the logo of Seats2meet.com as an **EPS (Encapsulated PostScript)** file and that's perfect. Logos should be vector images and we can transform the EPS to SWF to get a very sharp image in Prezi.

If for some reason, the organization you are working for doesn't have the logo in the EPS or **(Adobe Illustrator) AI** format, use a high resolution JPG or PNG. Make sure it's large enough; otherwise, it will look very ugly in your presentation. Never ever use a logo from the top-left corner of a company's website, as that's way too small. The logo should have a width or height of at least 1000 pixels. However, a vector-based format is recommended for a logo. More about vector-based formats is given in the following information box:

> Prezi is designed in Flash and Flash is based on vectors. The main advantage of vector images is that no matter how far you zoom in, the image is always sharp. Typical vector images are logos and illustrations. Vector images are usually made in Adobe Illustrator and will have AI or EPS extensions.
>
> It is possible to convert a vector image to a raster (pixel) image, but not the other way around. So, if you want a really sharp logo in your prezi, use a vector image.

We are lucky. Seats2meet.com has nice graphics available for our prezi. We got them as EPS files for our presentation.

We didn't have an office building as image yet, but Prezi has nice symbols in the library, and there's one available. It perfectly fits our needs.

Objective complete – mini debriefing

In the last step of our workflow, we defined the design issues for our presentation, such as the logo, what colors should be used, and whether there are specific fonts that need to be used. Nowadays, a lot of companies have a corporate style guide that has to be used as a basis for the presentation.

Creating your presentation

Now that we have already done so much work for our presentation, completing our presentation is really easy.

Prepare for lift off

Everything that should've been done, you did in the previous seven steps. So, now you have everything ready to create your prezi.

Engage thrusters

First, we transform the logo of Seats2meet.com from an EPS file to a SWF file. SWF files are the only vector files that Prezi can read. If you have AI files, you can work the same way and transform them to SWF files as well.

The following steps show you how to convert an EPS file to a SWF file using Adobe Illustrator. If you don't have an EPS or AI file, use a high resolution JPG or PNG file directly in Prezi and skip this step.

1. Open the EPS file in Adobe Illustrator.
2. Navigate to **File | Export**.
3. Choose the format option **Flash (swf)** and click on the **Export** button. Change the name of the file if necessary.
4. If you have other EPS or AI files, transform them to SWF as well.

Next, we go to `prezi.com` and start working on our prezi. In the following steps, we'll be working on the project we described in this project. Of course, you can use your own images and information based on your own storyboard.

1. Click on **New Prezi** on `prezi.com` and select **Start blank prezi**.
2. Delete all the objects on the canvas.
3. Navigate to **Insert | Symbols & shapes...** and select the **Photographic** category. Find the graphic of the office building and drag it to the canvas.
4. Then, insert the logo by navigating to **Insert | Images**. Make it the right size and put it on the office building.

Next, let's change the theme and choose our fonts and colors by performing the following steps:

1. Click on **Themes** and then click on the **Clear** style. Of course, you are free to pick another style.
2. Navigate to **Themes | Customize Current Theme** if you want to customize the style yourself and switch to mode **Advanced** if you want to enter colors as RGB codes.
3. Click on **Done** to leave the **Theme Wizard**.

Now, we're going create the windows where we can put our information. Perform the following steps:

1. Navigate to **Insert | Symbols & shapes...**, select the **Shapes** category, and draw a rectangle on the office building.
2. Click the rectangle on the canvas, click on **Style**, and choose a light color.

3. Make the rectangle the right size and position it on the office building; five windows should fit on one row.

4. If the first rectangle is positioned, click on it once and use the *Ctrl/Cmd + D* keys to duplicate it several times. Fine-tune the position of the windows.

5. Select all five windows by holding down the *Shift* key and dragging a rectangle around the windows, and then duplicate the windows with the *Ctrl/Cmd + D* keys to make more rows.

Our prezi now looks like the following image:

Now, put all the information, text and graphics, in the windows of the building. Make sure the information is in a logical order. After this, we will create the path and we don't want to make large jumps. We want the path to be smooth. In the first row, we place the information from left to right, in the second row from right to left, and in the third row again from left to right. This way, we won't have to make large jumps in our presentation.

Also, avoid large blocks of text. A few words is fine, but try to tell your story with as many images as possible. The result of our prezi so far is shown in the following screenshot:

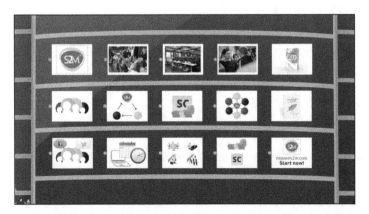

If everything is in the right position, create a path from window to window. Draw an invisible frame around the whole prezi. This will be your last path step; an overview of the complete prezi is shown in the following screenshot:

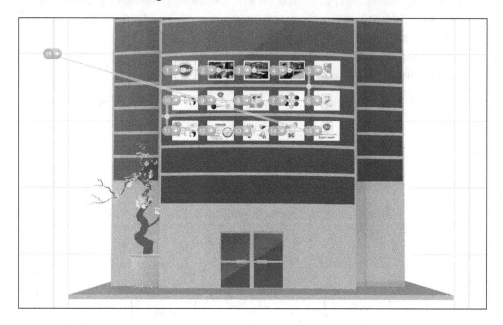

Finally, test your prezi.

Objective complete – mini debriefing

The last and final step for our business presentation is creating it. Because we did such a good job in preparing our presentation, this last step wasn't too hard. We only had to create it, and we didn't have to think about the content or design.

Classified intel

The final prezi we built wasn't very complicated. This is a good thing because we love simplicity. The most important thing is you followed the workflow. If you do a lot of thinking before doing, the doing part becomes really easy.

Mission accomplished

In this project, you learned how to use our seven-step workflow to get ready to build your business presentation in Prezi. First, we defined our strategy by describing the goal, the message, and the audience for our presentation. Next, we brainstormed the content and then we defined the three most important keywords. These keywords later became the subjects of our presentation. Then, we drew or described the creative concept. Usually, the creative concept is the overview of the prezi. In step five, we wrote down the story we want to tell on stage, and in step six we created a storyboard to visualize our story. The last step was defining the design elements like logo, fonts, and colors.

Finally, we created our presentation in Prezi. Watch it on www.prezihotshot.com. A final piece of advice: regularly look back at your strategy during your process and check whether you are still on the right track.

A Hotshot challenge

You don't only have to be creative if you are working on your presentation. Try to make it a habit to think visually. If you hear a story in your company or about another company, try to think of images to explain it. If you see specific words used in the organization, look them up in Google Images and see what shows up. If you are in a business meeting, you can try to translate certain words, processes, or stories to visuals. Visualization can create a new, interesting world for you!

However, let's leave business for now. Use the seven-step method to create a plan for the story of your life. Use your imagination and start writing and drawing!

Project 5

Presenting in the PechaKucha Style

PechaKucha is a whole new way of presenting. In 20 images and 20 seconds per image, the speaker shares his ideas, works, or thoughts. Two architects in Japan invented the concept because architects talk too much. PechaKucha is an ideal way of sharing your latest creative project, and it even could be the ideal way of shortening meetings because you have to get to the point immediately.

Mission briefing

In this project, you'll learn how you can use Prezi for your PechaKucha. Sometimes, we call it PreziKucha. First, we'll explain what PechaKucha is exactly. Next, we'll show you how you can use Prezi for it, and then we'll talk about images and where to get them.

Then, we are going to build a prezi for a PechaKucha about one of our holiday trips. Holidays are most fun to share and we can talk about them forever. So, it is a good exercise to talk about our holiday in just 6 minutes and 40 seconds. Finally, we'll give you some creative ideas to get more out of Prezi for your PechaKucha.

Why is it awesome?

Lots and lots of presentations take way too much time. PechaKucha could be an ideal way to shorten presentations and get focused. If you have only 6 minutes and 40 seconds, you can't dwell upon all kind of details that don't matter. It gives you just enough information and gives an opening entrance to further discussions and conversations.

Besides that, PechaKucha is a fun and inspirational format. It's fun to share your thoughts and ideas in PechaKucha format. You don't have to be an experienced speaker to give a PechaKucha. PechaKucha is a great new way of presenting what's on your mind. PechaKucha is for everyone.

Your Hotshot objectives

The major tasks to complete this project are:

- ▶ Understanding PechaKucha
- ▶ Using PechaKucha in Prezi
- ▶ Using images
- ▶ Presenting your idea in PechaKucha style
- ▶ Using your creativity

Mission checklist

There are no special requirements for this project, only twenty nice pictures to support your story.

Understanding PechaKucha

This task describes what PechaKucha is and where it comes from. It's important to know and understand this to use PechaKucha to it's full potential.

Engage thrusters

PechaKucha is a new form of presenting—showing 20 images that each remain on screen for 20 seconds as shown in the next illustration. The transition of the images is done automatically, and therefore a PechaKucha presentation lasts exactly 6 minutes and 40 seconds.

Astrid Klein and Mark Dytham invented the concept in 2003. They share a bureau for design and architecture in Tokyo, Klein Dytham architecture (KDa). They organized the first PechaKucha Night to provide young designers with an opportunity to meet, to network and see each other's work. Because of the limited time, the participants are forced to present in a short and simple way and this provides a chance for more people to present themselves. As an audience, it is easier to stay focused, because the presenters do not get the time to elaborate on all kinds of details that do not really matter.

PechaKucha is pronounced like a single word (petsha-kutsha). On Klein and Dytham's website, we read that PechaKucha is Japanese for the sound of conversation. This can be interpreted like the sound of dialogue, but we also find translations like tittle-tattle, babbling, and chitchat.

PechaKucha Nights have spread over more than 500 cities worldwide. At first, PechaKucha Nights were held for the most part by designers, artists, and architects, but a PechaKucha can be about any subject and anybody can participate. The participant is free to do whatever they want with images and story. On the international site of PechaKucha, `www.pechakucha.org`, you can check out a large number of PechaKuchas.

PechaKucha Night is trademarked to protect the hard work of the organizers of PechaKucha Nights. Each PechaKucha Night is run by a city organizer only for the inspiration, love, and fun of it. Mostly these people work in the creative industries. PechaKucha Nights are for content, never for profit.

The global PechaKucha network is organized and supported by Klein Dytham architecture.

Objective complete

In this section, you learned what PechaKucha is exactly, where it comes from, and it use. Use this information to get the most out of your presentation and start using PechaKucha to share your ideas and work.

Using PechaKucha in Prezi

In this task, we'll describe how you can use PechaKucha style in Prezi. Prezi has a separate option for it. PechaKucha in Prezi is great because you can take advantage of Prezi's zooming options to emphasize specific parts and give overview by zooming out. Besides that, Prezi has much more layout possibilities because you work on one large canvas. You can use your creativity to create a presentation that people will remember.

Engage thrusters

Prezi is prepared for PechaKucha style presenting. You can put Prezi on automatic playing so that you don't have to worry about the presentation anymore. You can fully concentrate on your story and the correct timing.

In short, you perform the following steps to present with Prezi in PechaKucha style. Details of how to create you prezi in PechaKucha style will be explained in the next paragraphs.

1. First, you put 20 images on the canvas by navigating to **Insert | Image**.
2. Then, you add every image to the path.
3. Finally, you present with the autoplay option of 20 seconds (in the bottom-right corner of your screen) as shown in the next screenshot:

   PechaKucha plays!

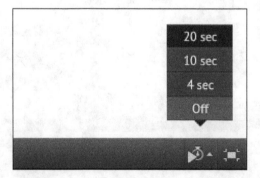

Objective complete – mini debriefing

It's easy to use PechaKucha style in Prezi. Just put twenty images in a path and select autoplay of 20 seconds.

Using images

In a PechaKucha, you have to use twenty images. You could use some text as well, but it's better to use just images. When you use text the audience starts reading and they will pay less attention to you and your story. The focus should be on you and the image should support your story, not the other way around. Another advantage of images is they can touch emotions and pull people in your story. Added text will only distract them. We'll explain in this task where you can get good pictures.

Engage thrusters

There are many ways to get good pictures. Roughly, the options are:

- Hire a photographer
- Buy high quality pictures
- Make your own pictures
- Collect pictures from the Internet

The first option is very expensive and requires good planning. You won't use this option for your PechaKucha. The second option is an easy one. You only have to pick, pay, and use. The pitfall of stock pictures is that the audience recognizes them as stock pictures. Maybe they are too perfect. For PechaKucha, the best option is to make your own pictures. There are three reasons for this: it's cheap, personal, and fun.

The audience wants you to tell your personal story. This works best if your pictures are also personal. Made by you.

Nowadays, everyone has a mobile phone. The quality is (mostly) very good, so you can use these pictures for your presentation without any doubt.

It's even more fun to use your own pictures for your presentation than those beautiful stock photos because your own pictures are more personal and even the not-so-perfect-shots are nice to watch. It's also much cheaper and you have nothing to do with copyright (because you have the copyright over these pictures), which makes it much easier.

The last option is to download pictures from the Internet. It's a good alternative, but it's tricky. You have to make sure you don't violate any copyright rules. It's not always visible if you can use a particular picture.

Though your own photos may not be perfect, that doesn't mean they should be of low quality. Make sure a picture has a width of height of at least 1000 pixels. Then the quality is good enough to show the photo fullscreen. This is easy to test on your own computer screen. If the image is still sharp when it fills your entire screen, it will be sharp during the presentation. You can also check the width and height of the image by clicking on the right mouse button and choosing **Properties** (for Windows) or **Get Info** (for Mac).

Objective complete – mini debriefing

For PechaKuchas, it's a good idea to use your own personal photos. It's cheap, personal, and good fun. Use photos of at least 1000 pixels wide/high.

Classified intel

If you give a lot of presentations and you like using personal photos, it's probably worthwhile to take a photo course to improve your own photos.

Presenting your idea in the PechaKucha style

Now, we will create our PechaKucha in Prezi about our last summer's holiday.

Prepare for lift off

First, we'll collect at least twenty images of our vacation to Croatia. We've taken quite a few pictures with our mobile phone, so we search for twenty to thirty pictures and copy them to our computer. We picked a few more so that we can decide inside Prezi which pictures fit best.

Engage thrusters

Open a new prezi, choose the blank template, and delete all the objects on the canvas. Make sure your canvas is completely empty.

Navigate to **Insert** | **Image** and choose all the pictures you have already selected. Prezi puts the images automatically in a grid. Choose multiple pictures while holding down the *Shift* key when you click on them, as shown in the following screenshot:

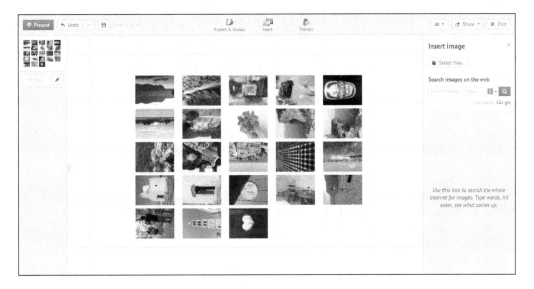

As you can see in the previous screenshot, not all pictures have the right position. Some pictures are upside down and some should be portrait. This could especially happen we you use pictures from your mobile phone.

Use the transformation tool to rotate the pictures that should be rotated. Hold down the *Shift* key while rotating to rotate around exactly 90 or 180 degrees. You can see the result in the next screenshot:

Now, let's arrange the pictures in the right order. The first and the last image are very important, the rest is just filling in. We chose the cut-out heart as the first picture because we want to start our holiday story with a *family-thing* and a heart that symbolizes love. In between, we want to show all kind of nice pictures to tell our story, and we also want to show some fun pictures. Make sure you choose exactly twenty pictures. Delete the pictures you don't need.

We want our PechaKucha to end with the subject we started our presentation with, which is family. So, we have chosen the picture with our kids asleep in the back of the car as the last picture. We thought that it's a nice picture to end our PechaKucha.

In Prezi, we put the pictures in the right order, five in a row. But note this! After the first row, we don't start at the beginning of the second row; we start from the end of the second row and work our way back to the beginning. The third row starts at the beginning and in the fourth row we start from the end again. We do this to avoid large steps in our path and to get a much more fluent flow in our presentation.

The problem we had with our pictures is that if we add these pictures to the path, not all the pictures get a good position. This is probably due to one of the settings, because they were taken with a mobile phone. Maybe you won't have this problem with your pictures and you can add them straight to the path, but we had to use invisible frames. Invisible frames are also great when you are determining the a part of the picture you want to show, especially when your picture is in portrait mode.

Draw an invisible frame with ratio 4:3 (by holding down the *Shift* key) and as large as one of the landscape pictures. Copy (*Ctrl/Cmd + C*) and paste (*Ctrl/Cmd + V*) the picture a few times and place them over the other pictures. You can also use the *Ctrl/Cmd + D* keys to duplicate the invisible frame.

Now, add all the invisible frames to the path. If you don't want to use invisible frames, you can add all the pictures to the path in the right order, as shown in the following screenshot:

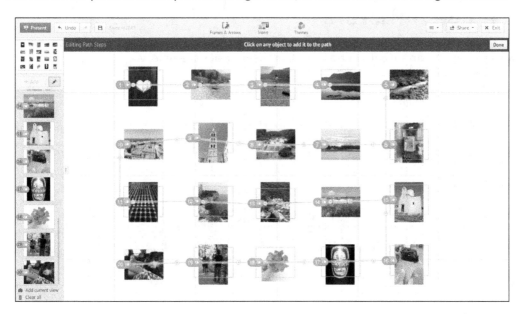

As you can see, the flow of the presentation is from left to right in the first row, from right to left in the second row, from left to right again in the third row, and finally from right to left in the fourth row. We are finished with our prezi.

Click on **Present** to test your PechaKucha. First, walk through it by clicking the arrows in the bottom of the screen or using the arrow keys on your keyboard. When you think the order is okay, test the PechaKucha by holding down the **Autoplay** option and choosing **20 sec**.

Objective complete – mini debriefing

We've created our first PechaKucha of our holiday pictures. We inserted photos onto the canvas, put them in the right order, and added them to the path. We used a simple raster pattern to put the photos in it.

Using your creativity

We already created a very simple PechaKucha. Just twenty images in a simple order and that's it. You can do more with Prezi if you want and if it adds something to your presentation. See if you can find a way to enhance your PechaKucha and make it memorable. You can watch our examples at www.prezihotshot.com.

Engage thrusters

We'll show you some different examples you can use for PechaKucha in Prezi and some ideas you can try. You can try different patterns. In the previous example, we used a grid. But you can also use the following:

- Horizontal line
- Vertical line
- Circle

Besides patterns, you can also use the zooming features of Prezi for your PechaKucha. For example:

- ▸ Zooming out at the end to reveal the last image
- ▸ Zooming out at the beginning to have a surprising start
- ▸ Zooming in to show details. Resolution of the pictures should be high
- ▸ A big rotation to show the opposite (don't use this too often)

We put three examples of PreziKuchas online at www.prezihotshot.com. The first one uses a grid as explained in detail in this project. The second one uses a circle as a pattern. The third one uses a big zoom-out to reveal the last image. In this case, the last image is the heart-shaped hole in the door. All the other images are placed in a heart-shaped pattern inside that hole.

Objective complete – mini debriefing

In this task, we explained how you can use a bit more creativity in your PechaKuchas by using another pattern instead of a grid and by using other transformations like rotating and zooming. It's not necessary, but it might suit your presentation.

The concept of a PechaKucha presentation is easy to understand, but you should practice before you can give a PechaKucha. Experience what it means to talk in a rhythm of 20 seconds. At first it might feel strange, but if you know your story (and you should because it's a personal story), you will notice (hopefully) it not that hard as it seems. Please don't worry too much about the 20 seconds. Don't wait for the next image if you're done with an image too early, just keep on talking. When you will be talking way too long about an image, consider splitting the image in two images or rethink your story about that particular image. To conclude, don't practice just once, practice a few times.

Mission accomplished

In this project, we used Prezi to create a PechaKucha style presentation. First, we learned what PechaKucha is and where it originates from. Then, we learned more about the images that we can use for our PechaKucha and where to get them. Finally, we created our PechaKucha with Prezi as shown in the following screenshot:

A Hotshot challenge

Reuse your PechaKucha, and ask someone to record your PechaKucha on video. Use the audio to create a voice-over for your prezi. Play the PechaKucha with the audio, record it as a movie, and put it on YouTube.

Project 6

Presenting Boring Stuff in a Better Way

Maybe it's a better idea not to present boring stuff at all!

But, what we mean here is the way data usually is presented is very boring and there is a better way to do it.

Mission briefing

In this project, you will learn how to present data in a much better way than you probably used to till now. In this project, our challenge is to make data visually attractive.

Our starting point is an Excel sheet with data. First, we'll show you what most people do and why that doesn't work.

Then, we'll show you what you can do to improve your graphs and make your data visually more attractive. We'll also show how you can visualize other kind of data, such as locations, chronological events, and pros and cons, as shown in the following screenshot:

Finally we'll put it all together in one prezi.

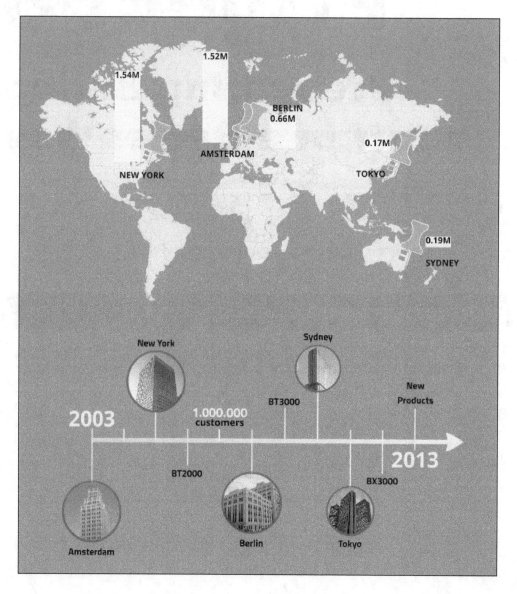

Why is it awesome?

Everyday, a lot of boring presentations are presented. Especially when it comes to financial data, for a lot of people it's not easy to make it look attractive. Lots of presentations are full of tables and graphs with too much information; information that can't be read because it's displayed too small, and information that doesn't matter at that moment.

In this project, we'll teach you how you can turn boring tables and graphs with data into something interesting and good looking. The data should support your story, not kill it.

Your Hotshot objectives

The major tasks to complete this project are as follows:

▶ Rethinking your data

▶ Creating great graphs

▶ Visualize locations

▶ Making interesting timelines

▶ Limiting your lists

▶ Put it all together

Mission checklist

You don't need anything special for this project. All you need is Excel and Prezi.

Rethinking your data

In this task, we'll show you what most people do to visualize data and why that doesn't work.

Prepare for lift off

To have data to work with, we put some financial and user data in an Excel sheet.

Engage thrusters

Data usually consists of lots and lots of numbers. You wouldn't be able to understand the data in one glance. You have to analyze the data, combine it, and compare it. You have to look for the differences and similarities.

A lot of people find this very difficult and if you have to do it during a presentation, it's even worse. The data might not be boring at all, but the way of presenting is boring because it's too hard to find out what those numbers mean. Consider the following screenshot:

Sales volumes 2012 & 2013

2012	Q1	Q2	Q3	Q4
New York	$279.382	$340.939	$320.393	$430.049
Amsterdam	$229.438	$183.729	$382.922	$569.822
Tokyo	$19.492	$20.393	$17.392	$23.039
Sydney	$34.929	$31.039	$35.030	$56.002
Berlin	$18.292	$560.295	$102.939	$135.281

2013	Q1	Q2	Q3	Q4
New York	$294.892	$430.939	$432.932	$376.249
Amsterdam	$234.928	$378.924	$429.483	$478.204
Tokyo	$34.879	$25.987	$56.783	$48.937
Sydney	$45.928	$44.029	$54.265	$48.736
Berlin	$139.553	$176.404	$168.473	$172.847

Numbers are boring. That's why people often use graphs. Graphs come in many styles such as line charts and bar charts.

With Excel, it's very easy to convert a table with data into a nice graph. The next two images represent sales volumes of 2012. The second graph also includes the total sales per quarter. This gives you new information and could be very interesting, but it also gives you a different graph. These kinds of decisions are very important and you should think about it very carefully because this can make a big difference in the way the audience interprets the information.

In the two next two screenshots, we will show the sales volumes of 2012, but maybe it's more interesting to compare the total sales volume of 2012 with the total sales volumes of 2013.

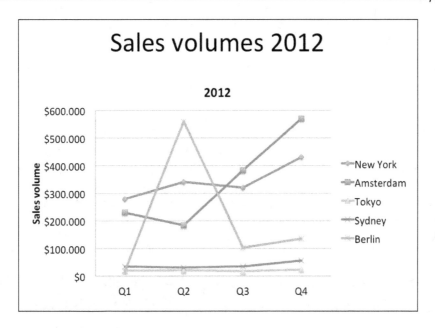

Maybe it's even more interesting to compare the total sales volumes of the different locations.

It's not just about the numbers, but we have to actually think very carefully about them and how they can be presented. Think really carefully about what you *want* to show and then decide *how* you want to show it.

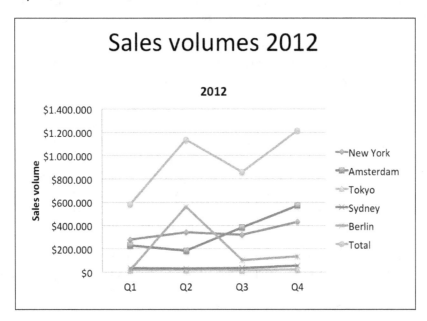

Maybe it's time to rethink your data. Of course, you have to look at the story you want to tell your audience and how can the numbers help you with this?

You don't have to show all the numbers. You only want to show the numbers that add value to your story or explain your story. You can put all the other numbers in the handout.

Objective complete – mini debriefing

In this task, we explained that *just numbers* are very boring and it's a very good idea to convert these numbers into a graph. You can use all kind of graphs, but it's very important to decide what you want to show and how you want to show it. That's why you have to rethink your data and have a (new) look at the story you want to share. What do you want to say actually? How can *the numbers* help you with it?

It's not very difficult to create a graph. However, it's a challenge to create a great graph.

Creating great graphs

Everyone can create a graph (at least we think everyone can), but how can you create a really great graph? We'll show you in this task.

Engage thrusters

So, what makes a great graph? We think a great graph is a graph that contains just enough information (less is more!) and is visually attractive.

Let's create a graph to compare the total sales volumes of 2012 with the total sales volumes of 2013. We used Microsoft Excel for this. First, we selected the table we want to convert to a graph. Then, we chose the **Charts** tab, the type we wanted (**Line**), and the subtype of **Line Charts**. We chose the most simple line chart. Excel did the rest for us and created a nice line chart.

However, we can do better than that. When you have a good look at the chart, you can see that the numbers on the left-hand side won't be readable in a large screen. We could make them bigger and abbreviate them to 1.2M instead of 1,200,000. However, if we want to compare the numbers of 2012 with 2013 and see which quarters were worse and which quarters were better, we don't need the numbers. Then, we only need the red and blue lines. Depending on which line is above the other, we can easily see which quarter was the best.

We are not saying that you always have to use only the lines of the graph in your presentation. It depends on what you want to communicate. Think about this very carefully.

It also depends on what you will say when you present this graphs. If you don't want to say anything and let the audience figure out themselves what the graph means, you can add some details. However, usually you will explain to the audience what they see, so the graph can be very simple and plain.

 If you want to use a graph in Prezi, make sure you save the image as PDF. The lines will be vectors, and if you want to zoom in to the chart, you won't see any blurry pixels.

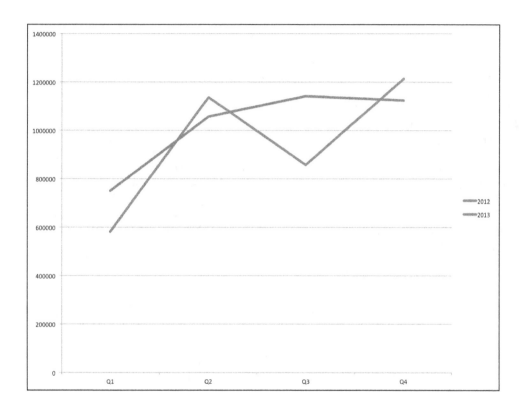

A standard Excel graph

The improved graph will look like the following screenshot:

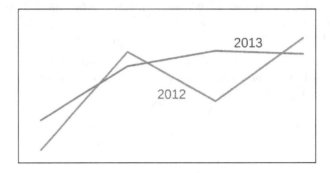

A minimalized graph with numbers added in Prezi

There's another way to use the numbers of the sales volumes of 2012 and 2013. If you want to show the differences between the four quarters, you can use the absolute numbers or the percentages in combination with an up or down arrow.

The next screenshot gives the same information but it looks very different. We used green arrows when the sales volumes increased and red arrows when they decreased. We also matched the size of the arrows with the size of the increase or decrease.

The next screenshot was only for the total sales volumes, but you could create these numbers for the separate locations as well.

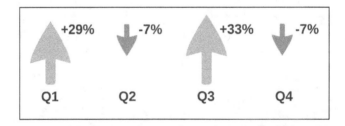

Finally, we want to share a very effective use of Prezi shapes to create bar charts. We'll show you how you can do this. Navigate to **Insert | Symbols & shapes | Shapes**. Drag one of the rectangles to the canvas, select the rectangle and duplicate it five times with the *Ctrl/ Command + D* keys, select one rectangle, and drag the top of the rectangle to give it the desired length. Repeat this for the other rectangles.

You can change the most important rectangle to a different color, and you can also add some numbers or some other information. Make sure you only add important information as shown in the next screenshot:

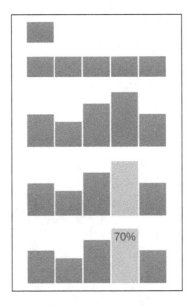

Objective complete – mini debriefing

It's easy to create a graph, but it takes a bit more time to first investigate what you exactly want to tell and then find out how you are going to show it. Make sure you only show what you want to tell. So, leave out the details from the graph to have more focus. Fewer details are easier to understand for your audience.

Visualizing locations

You might have noticed the company which we are using in this project has five locations: New York, Amsterdam, Tokyo, Sydney, and Berlin. If you want to talk about these five locations in your presentation, you can present them in a list, but why not make it a bit more visual?

Prepare for lift off

In this task, we'll be using an existing template of Prezi. You can use **World Map 1** or **World Map 2**. You can find these templates in the **Classic** category.

Engage thrusters

1. Go to **Your prezis** and open a **New prezi**.

2. Choose the template category **More** and select either **World Map 1** or **World Map 2** as shown in the following screenshot:

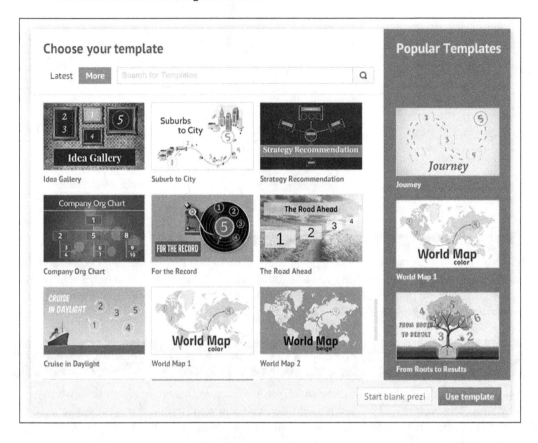

3. Delete the existing path from the prezi and remove all the unnecessary objects.

4. Navigate to **Insert | Symbols & shapes...** and choose (for instance) the category **Stickers**. Drag a pin to the world map. Position the pin to a location, make it the right size, and rotate it a bit. Select it and duplicate it four times with the *Ctrl/Command + D* keys. Also position the other pins, as shown in the next screenshot.

You can use all kind of symbols to visualize locations. The most commonly used symbols are pins, flags, and markers.

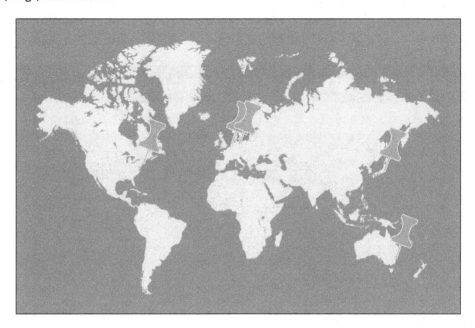

If it adds value, you can add additional information to the pins, for instance, the sales volumes per location for 2013.

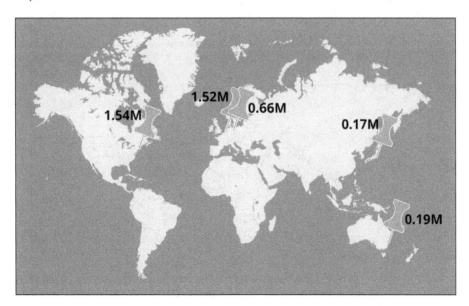

Objective complete – mini debriefing

Locations are perfect for visualization. You can use a world or country map for it. Just place pins, flags, or markers on the map and you're done. You could add some additional information such as the office names, the sales volume per locations, or other valuable information.

Making interesting timelines

Corporate presentations often contain a short history of the company. If it adds value to your story, we think it's a great idea. However, it should not be in a boring list, please! Use a timeline for it.

The following is the timeline we want to visualize:

- ▸ 2003: Our first office in Amsterdam
- ▸ 2005: New office in New York
- ▸ 2006: Launching BT2000
- ▸ 2007: 1.000.000 customers
- ▸ 2008: New office in Berlin
- ▸ 2009: Launching BT3000
- ▸ 2010: New office in Sydney
- ▸ 2011: New office in Tokyo
- ▸ 2012: Launching BX3000
- ▸ 2013: Complete new product range

Engage thrusters

Let's create a nice timeline.

 You could use a predefined Prezi timeline. You can find it by navigating to **Insert | Diagrams**. However, in this task, we will create the timeline ourselves.

1. Open a new blank prezi and remove everything from the canvas.
2. Navigate to **Frames & Arrows | Draw Arrow** and draw a large arrow from left to right on the canvas.
3. Instead of an arrow, you could also use a line. For timelines, we like to use arrows. It implies that there's more to come because it points to the future.

4. Now, draw 10 short lines perpendicular to the arrow and add the year numbers 2003 and 2013 to the beginning and end, as shown in the following screenshot:

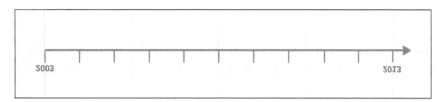

5. Now, you can start filling the timeline with frames and text, as shown in the following screenshot:

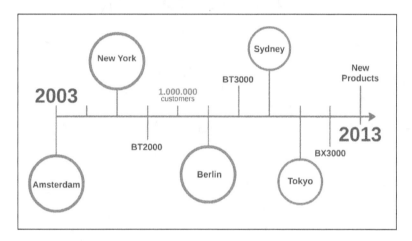

6. It's even better if you have nice pictures to add to the timeline, as shown in the following screenshot:

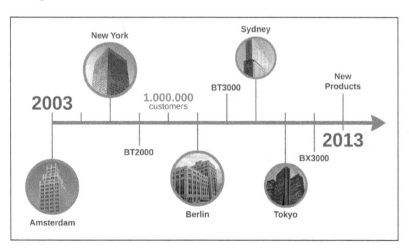

Objective complete – mini debriefing

In this task, you learned it's much more interesting to create a nice visual timeline instead of a boring list of historical facts.

Limiting your lists

In this task, we'll show you how to handle (long) lists. We've found an interesting slide that is an example of how it shouldn't be done.

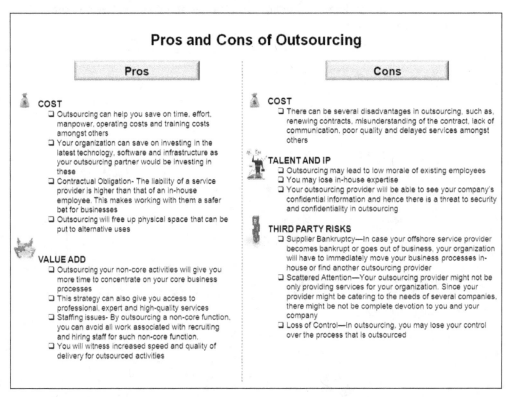

This is not the way to go!

Engage thrusters

Most presentations consist of slides full of bullets. Apparently, people are afraid to forget something, so why not put everything you know or you might want to say in a long list. The truth is, these lists add no value to your presentation. Also, the example slide we found has too much information.

Something is of added value if you can limit the content. Our advice is to limit your lists to a maximum of three. If you think the rest of the list is important too, put it in a handout.

If you have a list of specifications, just mention the three most important ones. For example, the three specifications that make your product unique. Don't mention the most obvious specifications such as *good quality*.

Another good way of using lists is to show pros and cons. Again, a maximum of three pros and a maximum of three cons should be used, as shown in the following screenshot. It's also okay to show just one of each.

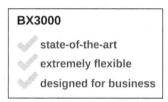

Try to make use of visual elements like a checkmark for pros and a red cross for cons as shown in the next screenshot. Since Facebook, you can also use a thumbs up for pros and thumbs down for cons. You can find these symbols by navigating to **Insert | Symbols & shapes...** in the **Prezi editor**.

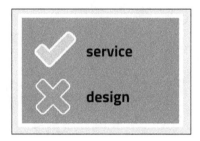

Objective complete – mini debriefing

In this task, you learned that you should never use long lists in your presentation. Use a maximum of three or even less. Use pros and cons to show the advantages and disadvantages. Again, use a maximum of three pros and and a maximum of three cons. Use well-known symbols to visualize something is right or wrong.

Putting it all together

We already showed a lot of possibilities of visualizing data. Now, let's put it all together in one prezi.

Prepare for lift off

The basis for this prezi is the **World Map 2** template. We used the prezi that we already created for our *Visualizing locations* task.

Engage thrusters

1. Go to **Your prezis** and open a **New prezi**.

2. Choose the template category **More** and choose **World Map 2**.

3. Delete the existing path from the prezi and remove all the unnecessary objects.

4. Navigate to **Insert | Symbols & shapes...** and choose the category **Stickers**. Drag a pin to the world map. Position the pin to a location, make it the right size, and rotate it a bit. Select it and duplicate it four times with the *Ctrl/Command + D* keys.

5. Also position the other pins, as shown in the following screenshot:

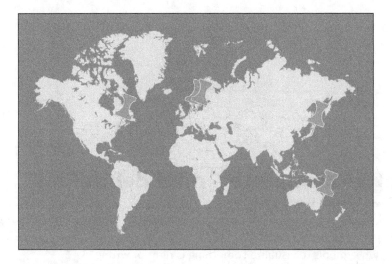

6. Navigate to **Insert | Symbols & shapes...** and choose the category **Shapes**. Drag a rectangle to the canvas and duplicate it four times. Positions the rectangle next to the pins. Select a rectangle and drag the top to give it the desired length. This visualizes the sales volume of that specific location. Repeat this for the other rectangles. Add the size of the sales volume in the rectangle in the form of text. Try to shorten the number. This result is shown in the following screenshot:

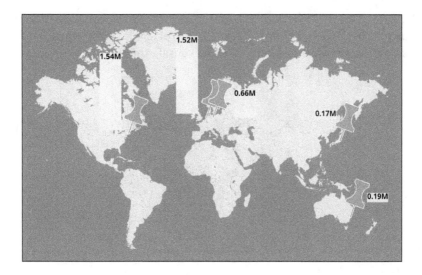

7. Now, let's add some detailed information.

8. Zoom into one of the pins.

9. Navigate to **Insert | Symbols & shapes...** and choose the category **Shapes**. Drag a rectangle on the canvas. Put the name of the location in the rectangle and at the left side the words `service`, `convenience`, and `added value`. We will add ratings for these subjects, so the audience can see how well (or badly) your business is doing.

10. Drag a circle to the canvas right after the word **service** and duplicate this circle four times. Now, you have five circles. Choose the filled circles for the value of the rating and empty circles for the rest. So, four filled circles means the rating is four out of five. Repeat this for the other subjects as shown in the following screenshot:

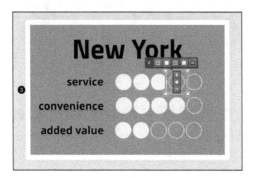

11. Place another rectangle under the first rectangle.

12. Navigate to **Insert | Symbols & shapes...** and choose the category **Stickers**. Drag the checkmark and the red cross in the rectangle. Write one advantage beside the checkmark and a disadvantage beside the red cross.

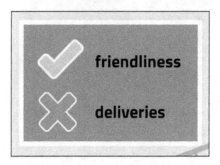

13. The last thing we'll add to our prezi is the timeline. We already created this in the *Interesting Timelines* task.

14. So, we'll copy and paste it to this prezi and change some colors so that it fits in with our template, as shown in the following screenshot:

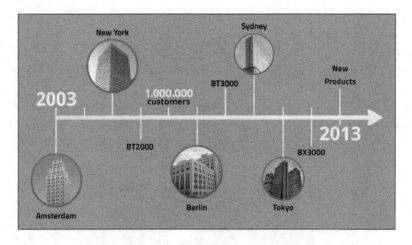

Objective complete – mini debriefing

In this task, we put everything we've learned into one prezi. It's the infographic way of presenting data. It's much more interesting to look at and much more fun to present.

Mission accomplished

In this project, we taught you how to present data in a better more attractive way.
It's important to not just show the numbers. Think carefully about what you want to show
and then decide how you want to show it. The numbers should support your story, not kill it.

We showed you how to create great graphs, visualize locations, create interesting timelines,
limit your lists, and visualize ratings. The following screenshot is an overview:

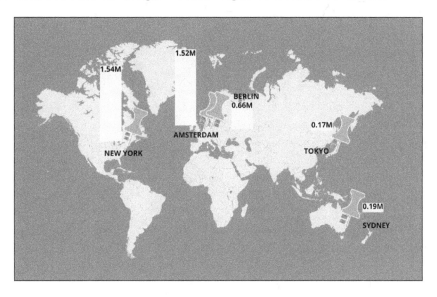

The following screenshot is a detailed view:

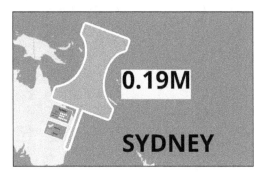

A Hotshot challenge

You can also use this infographic way of presenting your curriculum vitae. This is a perfect exercise to think about what's really important to share, what are your best skills, and how (for instance) you rate your language skills.

Rethink and create a fantastic infographic prezumé!

Project 7

I Really Like Those Hand-drawn Prezis

Maybe you have seen those really nice hand-drawn prezis and you were wondering how they were made? Did you ever think of creating them yourself?

We hear you say, "I can't draw." Well, we know you can. You might not be the greatest artist, but that's not necessary. We'll draw only simple objects. Drawings will help your audience to understand and remember your story. As children, visual thinking was natural to us. It's not lost, let's use it.

In this project, you'll see a few examples of hand-drawn prezis. You'll also find them on www.prezihotshot.com.

The first example is a prezi of TrendSketcher Anna Luise Sulimma. She created this for her speech on Prezi Day 2013.

The second example shows a prezi created for the Dutch Gymnastics Union:

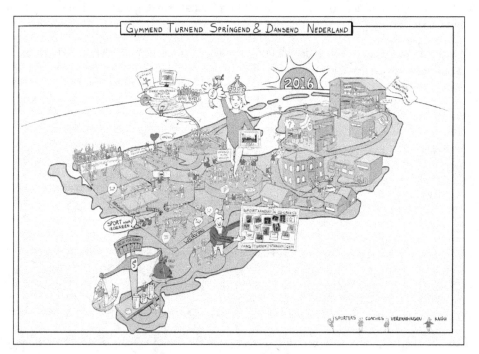

The third example is from learning futurist Maria Andersen's *The Future of Working*:

Mission briefing

In this project, we will teach you how to create your own hand-drawn prezis. We will not make it too complex, we'll leave that for the professionals.

We think simple drawings work the best, especially for Prezi. The idea is that drawing adds value (and some fun) to your story.

We have created the following story for our own prezi.

Sometimes, you have those days when everything seems to be negative—dark clouds arise above your head and there is lightning in your brain. You've lost overview; you don't know what to do. The reason—your head is too full. How can you get rid of these thoughts? How can you lighten up and be positive again? The following are five useful ideas:

- ▸ Go outside and dive into nature. Take a long walk in the woods and let the thoughts fly away.

- ▸ Write down everything that's in your mind.

- ▸ Start painting. It doesn't matter what it looks like, just throw your thoughts on the canvas.

- ▸ Try to rethink your thoughts. Is it really that bad? Can you change it? Can you get help for it?
- ▸ Smile! A big laugh helps you to be positive again.

Just five ideas to let the sun shine again, at least for today.

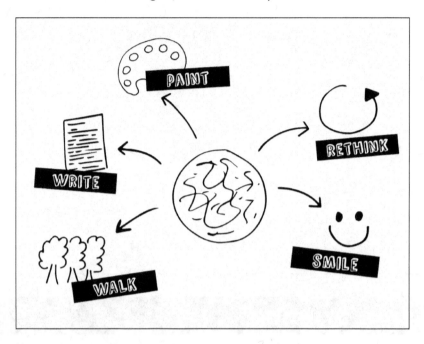

Why is it awesome?

Visual thinking is awesome. Visualizations in the forms of diagrams, pictures, and drawings help you to understand complex information. It's a way of organizing your thoughts to communicate more clearly. It's way of solving complex problems and thinking faster. Visual thinking is more natural to us than you might think. As children, we loved to draw. However, at some point in our life, we learned drawing is for artists. It's not. If you can draw a circle, triangle, rectangle, a line, an arc, and a dot, that's enough. With simple drawings, you can tell the best stories.

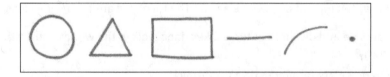

If you want to dive into visual thinking, read the book *The Back of the Napkin* by *Dan Roam*.

Your Hotshot objectives

The major tasks to complete in this project are:

- ▶ Let's draw!
- ▶ From a drawing to a vectorized image
- ▶ Putting it together in Prezi

Mission checklist

To vectorize our drawing, we'll need Adobe Illustrator. To create our drawings, we'll only need white paper and a pen, pencil, or marker.

Adobe Illustrator is used because it has the ability to export to SWF. We need SWF because of it's transparency capability. Most other software that create vectorized drawings can only export to a PDF, and a PDF is never transparent.

Alternatives to Adobe Illustrator are GIMP (`www.gimp.org`) and Inkscape (`www.inkscape.org`), but you'll need plugins to be able to export to SWF.

Let's draw!

Grab a piece of paper and marker and begin!

Prepare for lift off

We'll try to keep this part as simple as possible. We'll use plain white A4 paper and simple color markers. You could use fancy, expensive markers, but the markers used by kids work just fine.

Engage thrusters

The main idea for our story is to give five ideas to turn a negative, dark day into a positive, bright day.

We'll start by sketching very simple drawings. On the paper, put everything that pops up in your mind. If you wish to use a few words in your drawing, you can do so. However, try to draw as much as possible. Also, use as many pages as you need.

The following diagram is what our sketch looks like:

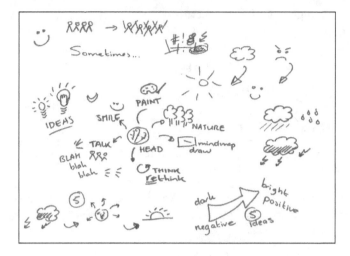

While sketching, we created our story. When we started, we didn't know what ideas we would generate and we didn't know we would end up with five ideas. While sketching, five ideas seemed a logical number. The only thing we knew before was that we wanted to turn something negative into something positive.

Now that we have the basic idea, we will put our story into a storyboard. This helps us to tell our story through visuals and helps us to know what drawings we'll need for our presentation.

The following diagram is our storyboard. As you can see, it consists of simple drawings only:

The next step is to draw the drawings we'll be using in our prezi. We created one drawing for the cloud with lightning.

As you can see in the next diagram, we have drawn lots of lightning. Later, we can find the best one and use that one in our prezi. So, your drawing doesn't have to be perfect. You can cut out what you don't need.

In the following diagram, you can see that we created one drawing for the five ideas:

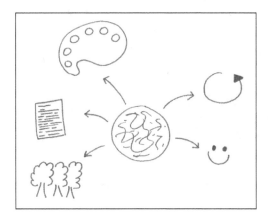

Also, we made one drawing for the Sun:

In the next step, we will convert these drawings to vectors and make separate drawings of each vector.

Objective complete – mini debriefing

In this task, we started with a brainstorm, drawing simple objects. Then, we created our storyboard. Again, we only used very simple drawings. When we knew what our story was, we drew our final drawings.

The next step is to vectorize our drawings.

From a drawing to a vectorized image

Before we can use our drawings in Prezi, we have to scan the drawings. All scanned drawings consist of pixels (squares). An image made of pixels is called a **raster image** or a **bitmap**. We could use them directly in Prezi, but the pixelated images won't look very nice. It's much nicer to vectorize our drawings.

Especially when you zoom in, you can clearly see the difference between a raster image and a vector image. It is shown in the following diagram:

First, we have to vectorize our scanned image. We will use Adobe Illustrator for This. Vector images are saved as an AI or EPS extension. However, we can't use these formats in Prezi. We need to convert the image to SWF. This is Flash's document format and, as Prezi was designed in Flash, this is the right format for vector images to use in Prezi.

Prepare for lift off

Before you can use your drawings digitally, you have to scan the drawings and save them as PDF, JPG, or PNG.

Engage thrusters

1. Open one of your drawings in Adobe Illustrator as shown in the following screenshot:

2. Your drawing should be rotated first.

3. Make sure the image is selected (just click on it) and navigate to **Object** | **Transform** | **Rotate**. Type in 270 degrees (in our case) and click on **OK**.

4. Navigate to **Object** | **Artboards** | **Fit to Artwork Bounds** to fit the image on the canvas, as shown in the following screenshot:

Now, the cool part starts. Let's vectorize!

5. Select **Image Trace** under **Window**.

6. If the options in the **Image Trace** dialog are grayed out, click once or double-click on the image one or more times.

7. There are a lot of options available, but we need to use only one important option. Make sure the **Mode** is set to **Black and White** and then click on **Trace**, as shown in the next screenshot:

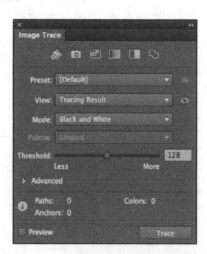

8. Now, click on **Expand** after navigating to **Object | Image Trace** and you are ready to use the vectorized image. This is shown in the following screenshot:

We need to create separate images for our prezi. This gives us more flexibility because we can position and scale the separate images and easily fit them in our design.

9. Select the **Lasso Tool** from **Toolbox**. You can also use the shortcut key *Q*.
Drag a lasso around the word **Sometimes...** as shown in the following screenshot:

10. As you can see, only the word **Sometimes...** will be selected now as shown in the following screenshot:

11. Press the *Ctrl/Command + C* keys to copy. Open a new image with *Ctrl/Command + N* or by clicking on **New** under **File** and then clicking on **OK** in the dialog. Paste the image on the canvas using the *Ctrl/Command + V* keys. Select **Fit to Artwork Bounds** under **Object | Artboards** to fit the image precisely on the canvas, as shown in the following screenshot:

We're almost finished. Now, let's export the file to SWF format.

12. First save the file as AI format, as you might need it later. Click on **Save as** under **File**, give the file a name, and click on **Save**. Click on **OK** in the next dialog box.

13. Now, select **Export** under **File**. Select the **Flash (swf)** format, give the file a name, and click on **Export**. Click on **OK** in the next dialog box. Usually, the default settings are fine.

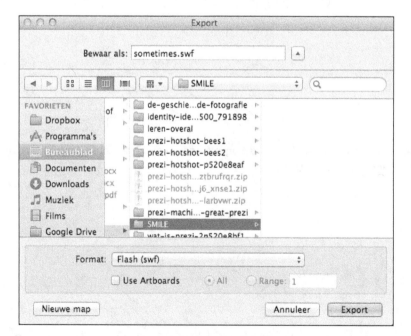

Do the same for the cloud and export it as a separate SWF file. If you drew more than one lightning arrow just like us, you can choose the best one and export that arrow as a SWF file. In Prezi, you can duplicate it for multiple uses.

Now, repeat this for the other drawings and save them all as separate SWF files. We separated the drawing with the five ideas into eleven images: the head, five arrows and the five ideas.

Objective complete – mini debriefing

In this task, we vectorized our drawings. First, we scanned our drawings and then used Adobe Illustrator to convert our pixelated drawings into nice vectors. The **Trace Image** feature did the job for us. We isolated the separate images and exported them to SWF. Now, let's put everything in Prezi and create our presentation.

Putting it together in Prezi

We have all the pieces ready now and are ready to create our presentation in Prezi.

Engage thrusters

Open a new blank prezi. Our presentation consists of three parts: the introduction with the dark cloud, the solution with five ideas, and the end with the sunrise. We'll put these parts vertically one below the other.

Let's start with the introduction. Insert the cloud, the word **Sometimes...**, and a lightning arrow. You probably have to resize the objects in Prezi. You can duplicate the arrow with the *Ctrl/Command + D* keys.

Your canvas should look like the following screenshot:

Now, we'll put two invisible frames on the canvas. One frame around the word **Sometimes** (that's where we'll start our prezi) and one frame around the whole picture. After we've showed the word **Sometimes**, we'll zoom out and add the other elements, as shown in the following screenshot:

First, add the small frame to the path and then the larger frame. Select all the lightning arrows (by pressing *Shift* and then clicking and dragging) and group them. Now, enter the path and click on the star of path step 2 to create a fade-in animation. First, click on the cloud and then on the arrows, as shown in the following screenshot:

Leave the path. The introduction is finished. The flow of the prezi you created so far is shown in the following screenshot:

Let's move on with the middle part of the presentation. Add the eleven drawings of the middle part to the canvas and position them nicely, as shown in the following screenshot:

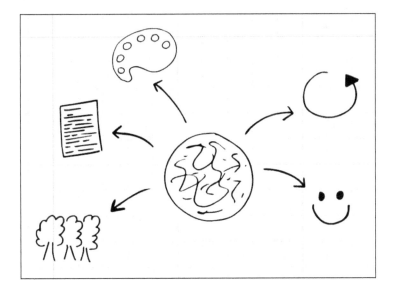

While working on this prezi, we got the idea to add labels to the ideas. Before we make the drawing of the full head (the circle) visible first, show the text **YOUR HEAD IS TOO FULL**.

We created the labels with a black rectangle and white text. We grouped the rectangle with the text before positioning it. We gave the labels with the text **YOUR HEAD IS TOO FULL** a small rotation so that it looks it a bit more playful.

If we put the circle on top of the center text, we will still see the text through because our vector drawings are transparent. To solve this, we created a plain white circle in Adobe Illustrator and exported it as SWF. Then, we put that circle behind the transparent circle and grouped it. Now, we can use fade-in animation to make the circle visible on top of the text **YOUR HEAD IS TOO FULL**, as shown in the following screenshot:

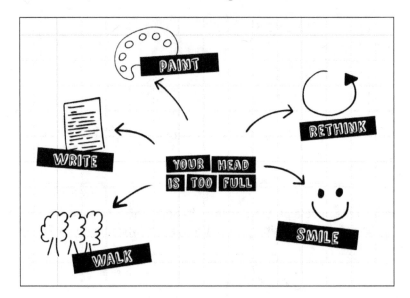

Add two invisible frames and add them to the path, as shown in the following screenshot:

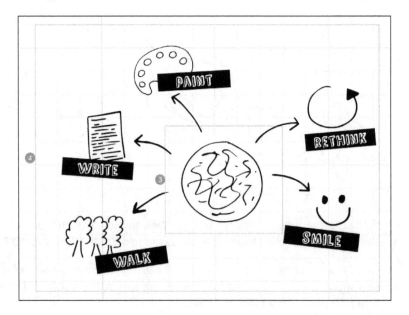

Use fade-in animation to create the right flow, as shown in the following screenshot:

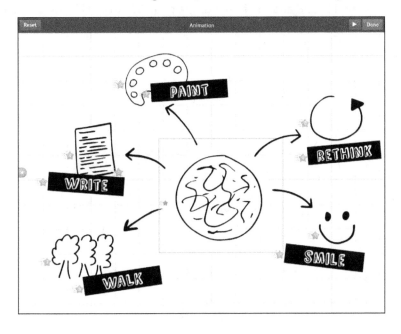

The last part is very simple. Just add the drawing of the sunrise to your canvas, draw an invisible frame around it, and add the frame to the path. We would like the two ends of the horizon to not be visible on screen, so we draw the frame a bit smaller. The whole prezi now looks like the following screenshot:

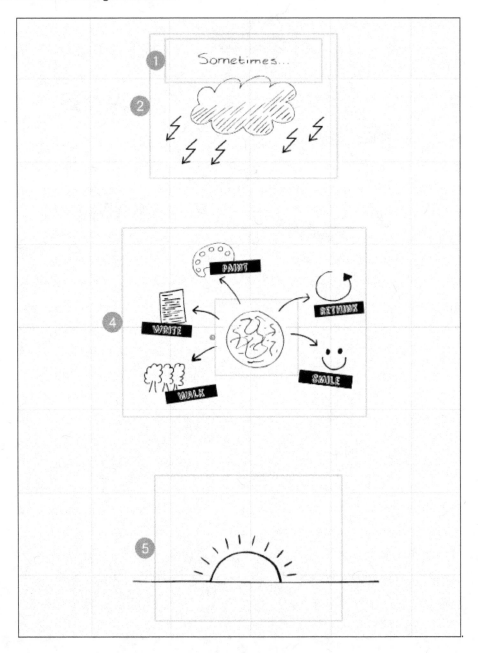

Objective complete – mini debriefing

In this task, we put all the small drawings together in one presentation. We did the last modifications of positioning and scaling in Prezi and we used invisible frames and fade-in animations to create a nice flow. Of course, you can view the prezi online at `www.prezihotshot.com`.

Mission accomplished

The goal of the project was to show you that drawing is easy and you can create great prezis with your own drawings.

We started this project by brainstorming and sketching on paper, and when we got our main idea, we created a storyboard for it. Then, we created the drawings we needed for the prezi.

We scanned the drawings, vectorized them with Adobe Illustrator, and inserted them in the prezi. Then, we positioned and scaled the drawings and we made a nice flow with invisible frames and fade-in animations.

Drawing made the sun shine in our prezi!

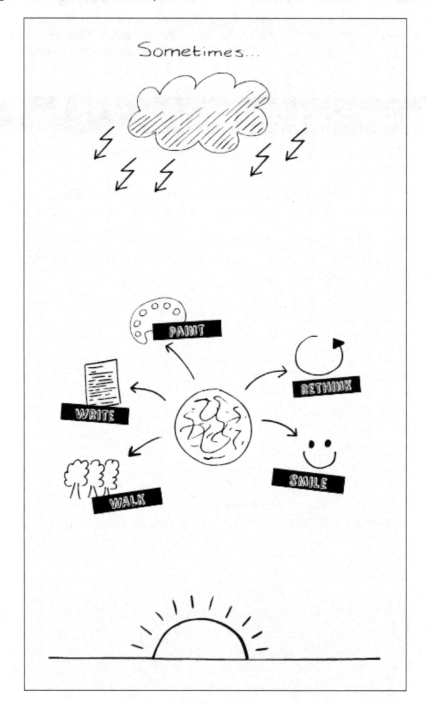

A Hotshot challenge

In this project, we only used black and white drawings. The simplicity of black and white drawings works very well in Prezi.

But, sometimes, color can do a great job for you. Color can give focus on certain parts of the presentation and spice up your prezi. Start experimenting with color in your drawings, but we want you to use just one color. You have two opportunities for this. You can use color in your drawings before you scan them or you can add *digital* color later with Illustrator or Prezi.

Project 8

Let's Animate Your Prezi

Now that you know everything about Prezi, it's time to move on and to learn how to create stunning Flash animations and use them in Prezi. Animations can bring your Prezi to life.

Mission briefing

When I wrote my second Prezi book in January 2012, *Presenteren met Prezi, Second Edition* (in Dutch), I wanted to create a really cool prezi as an example for the book. I had the idea of this specific prezi for over a year already. It took me a few nights to build it, but I loved doing it and I'm still happy with it. I got a lot of reactions from people who saw this prezi, and many people asked me how I did it. So, now it's time to dive into it and reveal it to you.

The idea of the prezi was to create a Prezi machine. The idea is simple: you put some information in the machine, a few things happen in the machine, and the output is a great presentation.

The style is cartoonish and funny, but carries a real message. I used animations to give the presentation the "wow factor".

Visit www.prezihotshot.com to view the prezi online.

The machine is shaking, clouds of smoke are popping out of the machine, and the gauge pointers are rotating, as shown in the following screenshot:

Why is it awesome?

Animations are cool. People love movement. Movement gives attention and focus and movement makes people smile—a smiling audience is better than a yawning audience.

With animations, you can make a big impression. In this project, we'll use animations for fun and to spice up our prezi. However, you can also use animations to explain information or to emphasize what you want to say. Animations are good for fun, but you can also overdo it. Be careful.

Your Hotshot objectives

The following are the major tasks that need to be completed in this project:

- ▶ Main idea – the Prezi machine
- ▶ Where do I get great illustrations?
- ▶ Building the basics
- ▶ Creating animations in Flash
- ▶ Putting it all together in Prezi

Mission checklist

In this project, we'll be using Adobe Flash Professional to create animations and Adobe Illustrator to do the artwork. We'll put all the pieces together in Prezi. We'll be using Adobe Creative Suite 6 (CS6) in this project; but if you have an older version, that's also fine. Maybe some screenshots will look slightly different.

If you don't have any Adobe software yet, you can download trial versions from `www.adobe.com`.

Main idea – the Prezi machine

Let's explain the main idea and create our story.

Engage thrusters

The Prezi machine is fantastic! You can put all kinds of information in it and if you use the machine the right way, a great presentation comes out, as shown in the following diagram:

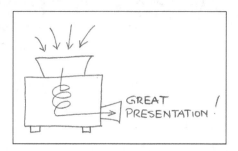

The question we want to answer in our presentation is *What makes a great prezi?*

Our story is as follows:

> *So... What makes a great prezi?*
>
> *Every prezi starts with a great idea.*
>
> *Put everything that pops up in your mind on the canvas.*
>
> *Do it with love and passion (because if you present a subject you don't like, it will fail immediately).*
>
> *Transform your brainstorm in a mind map and develop structure in your content.*
>
> *Then you'll need the Prezi machine. Make what's important big and the details small. Create groups of pieces of information that belong to each other.*

Get rid of the rubbish. That means: if a piece of information is not really important, leave it out. Remember: too much text will kill your presentation and bullets won't help you. Also, do you use rotation because you think it's fun?! (It's not.)

What you should do is: simplify.

Add images and videos.

But most of all: tell a story. Because, if you do tell a story it doesn't really matter if you use Prezi, PowerPoint, Keynote or some other tool.

A story makes a great presentation.

Objective complete – mini debriefing

Every great prezi should have a great story and that's how we started. Now that we know what message we want to share and what story we want to tell, we have to find or create the illustrations for our presentation.

Where do I get great illustrations?

If you're an artist, you should draw your own illustrations. However, most of you probably have no clue how to draw a nice illustration. Also, you don't have to. The Internet gives you loads of opportunities to find great illustrations. We'll show you how.

Prepare for lift off

In this project, we are going to create Flash animations. Flash is a vector-based program, so the illustrations we will use in this project should be vector-based images.

 In *Project 7, I Really Like Those Hand-Drawn Prezis*, we explained the difference between vector-based images and pixel-based images.

Engage thrusters

Our main idea is a Prezi machine, which means we have to find an illustration of a machine somewhere. Our favorite website for illustrations is iStockphoto.com. Using this website, you can not only find great photos, but also illustrations, videos, sounds, and even animations.

Go to www.istockphoto.com, type machine in the search field, and click on **Search**, as shown in the following screenshot:

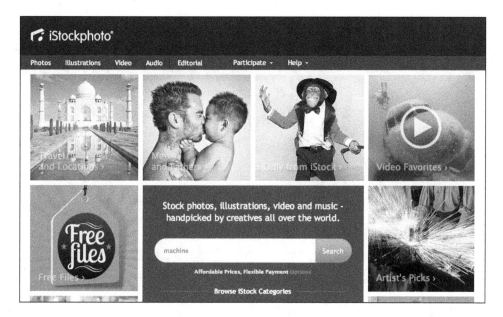

Open the drop-down menu besides the **Search** button, make sure only **Illustrations** is marked, and click on **Search** again, as shown in the following screenshot:

Find the illustration you want to use and click on it.

Make sure you have an account in iStockphoto.com (or create one) and buy the illustration—the illustrations are not free.

On www.prezihotshot.com, you'll find the direct link to the illustration we've used, as shown in the following screenshot:

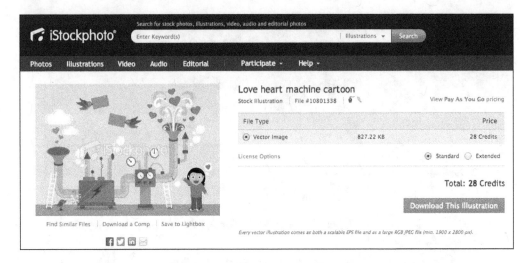

The downloaded file is a ZIP file and contains an .eps and a .jpg file.

We'll be using the .eps file for our project.

Objective complete – mini debriefing

You can draw your vector-based illustrations yourself (that would be awesome), but stockphoto sites are great to buy vector-based images.

Don't underestimate the time you need to find the right image. Sometimes, you'll find the right image in 5 minutes, while sometimes it takes a whole day. If you want to use Flash animations in your prezi, make sure you use vector-based images.

Classified intel

If you're not sure whether the illustration is the right choice for your project, you can first download a comp. This is the illustration with the watermark of **iStockphoto** in it. You can't use this in your final project, but you can first try the image before you buy it. On the iStockphoto site, you can find the **Download this illustration** button right under the illustration after you have chosen it (see the preceding screenshot).

Of course, `iStockphoto.com` is not the only stockphoto website. You can also try:

- ▶ `www.shutterstock.com`
- ▶ `www.dreamstime.com`
- ▶ `www.gettyimages.com`
- ▶ `www.123rf.com`
- ▶ `www.fotolia.com`

 If you want to learn how to create vector graphics yourself, read *Inkscape Beginner's Guide* or *Inkscape 0.48 Illustrator's Cookbook, Packt Publishing*.

Building the basics

Before we can start creating our animations, we have to build the basics first. The basics are all the illustrations we need for our prezi and the animations. We are not building one big illustration-animation file and putting that in Prezi. All the parts will be separate to make the prezi most flexible.

The following are the most important parts for our prezi:

- ▶ A happy girl
- ▶ A machine
- ▶ A machine with gauges
- ▶ Pipes
- ▶ Small parts such as clouds, hearts, and a bird with letter

Prepare for lift off

We'll be using the Adobe Illustrator for this task. Open the downloaded .eps file in the Adobe Illustrator, as shown in the following screenshot:

Engage thrusters

The happy girl asks an important question, so we'll start with her.

The happy girl

The happy girl is in the .eps file on a separate layer, let's first select and separate her. We will create the happy girl by performing the following steps:

1. Open the **Layers** panel by navigating to **Window | Layers**.

2. Open Layer 1 and <Group> to find the layer with the girl. Click on the circle present at the right side of the layer to select the girl. The girl is selected if you can see all the blue lines shown in the following screenshot:

3. Press *Ctrl/Cmd + C* to copy the selection, open a new file by navigating to **File | New** (just click on **OK** with the default values of the new file), and paste the selection of the girl in the new file by pressing *Ctrl/Cmd + V*.

4. Navigate to **Object | Artboards | Fit to Artwork Bounds** to trim the canvas.

5. Navigate to **View | Zoom In** to get a good view of the girl, as shown in the following screenshot:

We need to change the color of the heart and put it on the T-shirt, but the whole graphic is grouped. To solve this, we need to perform the following steps:

1. Navigate to **Object | Ungroup** and deselect all by clicking on the canvas.

2. Select the heart and navigate to **Object | Ungroup** again. Now, we can change the color of the heart. Click on the heart, navigate to **Window | Color**, and pick a nice color.

3. Rotate the heart a bit and put it on the shirt. To rotate move the mouse slightly off the squares of the selection box until a double-sided arrow appears. If you want, you can change the color of the T-shirt or trousers too.

4. Now, we want to flip the whole graphic vertical to put the outstretched arm to the other side.

5. Select the whole graphic by pressing *Ctrl/Cmd + A*.

6. Find the **Rotate Tool** in the toolbox (in the **Tools** panel), click and hold down the mouse, and choose **Reflect Tool**. Double-click on the **Reflect Tool**, choose **Vertical**, and click on **OK**. The whole image will be flipped, as shown in the following screenshot:

Our happy girl is finished, so let's save her as a .swf file. We'll need that for Prezi.

1. Navigate to **File | Export**.

2. Choose the **Flash (swf)** format, type the name girl.swf, and click on **Export**.

3. Click on **OK** present in the next screen. Save the original file of the girl as girl.ai, in case you want to makes changes later. Close the file, and you'll return to the .eps file of the whole machine.

The machine

1. Open the **Layers** panel again by navigating to **Window | Layers** and find the layer of the big machine. Select the layer by clicking on the circle behind the layer. Copy the machine and paste it in a new file.

2. Navigate to **Object | Artboards | Fit to Artwork Bounds** to trim the canvas.

3. Select the machine and navigate to **Object | Ungroup**. Deselect all, select the lighting sign, and delete it.

4. Navigate to **File | Save** as and save the file as `machine.ai`.

This file is ready to create an animation in the next task. We don't need it in the Adobe Illustrator anymore so close it now. The machine would look similar to the one shown in the following screenshot:

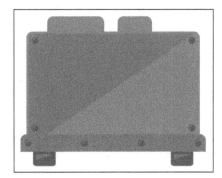

A machine with gauges

In the same way, we can separate the machine with gauges. If you want to animate other gauges as well, you should separate them too. We saved the files as `machine-gauges.ai`, `gauge3.ai`, and `gauge4.ai`. A machine with gauges would look similar to the ones shown in the following screenshot:

The pipes

The pipes of our machine consist of a lot of parts. It's easier to work the other way round and remove the parts we don't need.

1. First, we'll need to make a copy of the whole image.

2. Press *Ctrl/Cmd + A* to select the whole graphic and press *Ctrl/Cmd + C* to copy it. Open a new file and paste the graphic in it.

3. Remove all the parts you don't need for the pipe's file. It should look similar to the one shown in the following screenshot. Save it as `pipes.ai` and close it.

The small parts

We are almost done with the basics. We only have to create the `.swf` files for the rest of the small parts, such as clouds, hearts, and the bird with the letter. There are three different hearts: a blue, a pink, and a red one. We can create hearts of different sizes and rotations in Prezi. The same works for the clouds. If you can reuse your graphics, please do so.

We created `bird.swf`, `heart-blue.swf`, `heart-pink.swf`, `heart-red.swf`, and `cloud.swf`, as shown in the following screenshot:

Objective complete – mini debriefing

In this task, we separated our `.eps` file into smaller files with the Adobe Illustrator. We exported the static graphics as `.swf` files and the graphics to be animated as `.ai` files. The next step is to create the animations and then put it all together in Prezi.

Creating animations in Flash

Finally, we're ready to create the animations in Flash. It's the best part of all, so let's have some fun!

The following are the animations we'll be creating in this task:

▶ Moving the machine

▶ Popping out the smoke clouds

▶ Rotating the gauge pointers

 It's important to know that the Flash animations files will always have an infinite loop in Prezi.

Engage thrusters

It might seem difficult to create animations in Flash. I'll show you it's not that difficult at all!

Moving the machine

We can move the machine by performing the following steps:

1. Open Adobe Flash Professional and create a new empty file by navigating to **Create New | ActionScript 3.0**.

2. Navigate to **File | Import | Import to Stage**, choose `machine.ai`, and click on **Open**.

3. Set the **Convert layers to: Single Flash Layer** option and mark the following two options:

    - **Place objects at original position**

    - **Set stage size to same size as Illustrator artboard (172 x 136)**

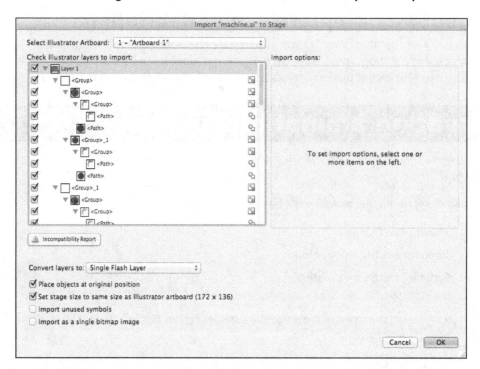

We need some extra space around the machine, so we will enlarge the canvas.

4. Navigate to **Modify | Document** and make the dimensions 10 pixels wider and 10 pixels higher. Put the machine in the middle of the canvas. It doesn't have to be the exact middle though.

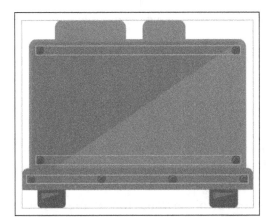

5. In the timeline, right-click on `frame 2` and choose **Insert Keyframe** or press *F6* on your keyboard. Hit the right arrow key to move the machine 1 pixel to the right.

6. Right-click on `frame 3` and choose **Insert Keyframe**. Hit the left arrow key to move the machine 1 pixel to the left.

7. Right-click on `frame 4` and insert another keyframe. Move the machine 1 pixel up.

8. Right-click on `frame 5`, insert a keyframe, and move the machine 1 pixel down.

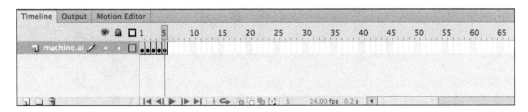

9. Press the *Enter* key to test the movement.

10. Save the file as `machine.fla`.

11. Use the combination keys *Ctrl/Cmd + Enter* to create the `.swf` file and to view the infinite loop. The `.swf` file will be placed in the same folder as the `.fla` file.

 If you think the machine should shake much more, move 2 pixels instead of moving 1 pixel.

Popping out the smoke clouds

We will use the `pipes.ai` file for our smoke animations. We will use the whole file because location of the clouds is easier that way.

We can pop out smoke clouds by performing the following steps:

1. Open a new empty Flash file and import `pipes.ai`. Use the same settings as for the machine import.

2. Click somewhere on the canvas to select the whole illustration (notice a small blue line around it) and navigate to **Modify | Break Apart**.

3. Deselect all the objects by pressing the *Esc* key or clicking somewhere on the canvas.

4. Create a new layer by clicking on the most bottom-left button in the timeline or by navigating to **Insert | Timeline | Layer**. Double-click on the layer and rename it as `cloud1_1`.

5. Select the smallest cloud of the clouds to the extreme left on the canvas (just click on it once).

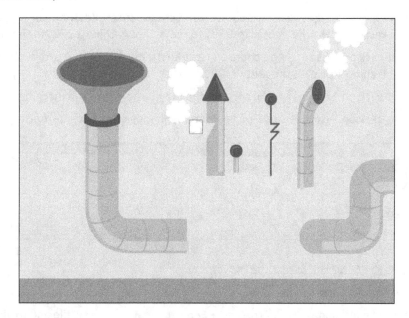

6. Press *Ctrl/Cmd + X*, click on the new layer, and navigate to **Edit | Paste in Place**.

7. Insert another two layers and name them `cloud1_2` and `cloud1_3`. Move the second cloud of the three leftmost clouds to the `cloud1_2` layer, and then move the third cloud to the `cloud1_3` layer. Use **Paste in Place** instead of the usual paste.

8. Right-click on `frame 10` present in the `cloud1_1` layer and choose **Insert Frame** or press *F5* on your keyboard. Now, the smallest cloud will be visible for 10 frames.

9. Click on the second cloud in the canvas and press *Ctrl/Cmd + X*. Right-click on `frame 10` in the `cloud1_2` layer and choose **Insert Keyframe**. Navigate to **Edit | Paste in Place** to put the second cloud back on the canvas.

10. Right-click on `frame 20` in the `cloud1_2` layer and choose **Insert Frame**. Now, the second cloud will be visible for the frame between 10 and 20.

11. Click on the timeline somewhere on `frame 1` and select the third cloud on the canvas. Choose *Ctrl/Cmd + X*. Right-click on `frame 20` in the `cloud1_3` layer and choose **Insert Keyframe**.

12. Navigate to **Edit | Paste in Place** to put the third cloud back on the canvas.

13. Right-click on `frame 30` in the `cloud1_3` layer and choose **Insert Keyframe**. Now, the third cloud will be visible for the frame between 20 and 30.

14. To make the rest of the illustration visible in all frames, right-click on `frame 30` in the `pipes.ai` layer and choose **Insert Frame**.

The timeline should look similar to the following one:

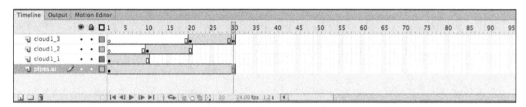

It's nice if the large cloud fades out and there's a pause at the end of the animation so that it doesn't start over again right away.

15. Right-click on `frame 30` in the `cloud1_3` layer and choose **Create Motion Tween**. Click on **OK** to the question **Do you want to convert and create a tween?**

16. Right-click on `frame 40` in the `cloud1_3` layer and navigate to **Insert Keyframe | All**.

17. Click on `frame 40` in the timeline, then click on the third cloud on the canvas, open the **Properties** panel, and choose the **Alpha** option in the **Color Effect** menu. Put the slider to 0%.

18. Now right-click on `frame 85` in the `cloud1_3` layer and choose **Insert Frame**.

19. Also, right-click on `frame 85` in the `pipes.ai` layer and choose **Insert Frame** again. The timeline should look similar to the following one:

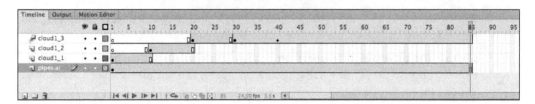

20. Save the file as `pipes.fla` and press *Ctrl/Cmd + Enter* to create and view the `.swf` file so far.

Now, let's move the second set of clouds to the middle of the machine. This explanation will be shorter. The following are the steps that needs to be performed:

1. Delete the smallest of the three clouds.

2. Create two new layers `cloud2_1` and `cloud2_2` and move the clouds to these layers.

3. Now create the animations. The smallest cloud should be visible from frame 15 till frame 25 and the other one from frame 25 till 35.

4. If you paste a cloud in a new frame, the cloud will be visible automatically till frame 85. For the `cloud2_1` layer, remove the frames after `frames 25` and for the `cloud2_2` layer, remove the frames after frame 35.

5. For this animation, you don't have to create a fade out. Not every animation should be the same. Clouds don't behave the same either.

So far, the timeline will look like the following screenshot:

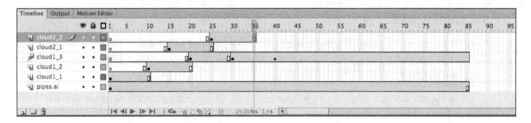

Do you think you can create the last cloud's animation by yourself? Make it almost the same as the first animation, with a fade-out effect for the last cloud. We deleted one of the smallest clouds, so three clouds are left.

The timeline would look as follows:

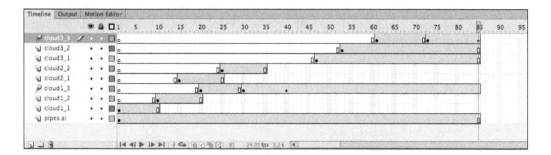

 All kinds of variations are possible for these kind of animations. Use your imagination and experiment a lot!

Rotating gauge pointers

Ready for the last set of animations? Let's animate a few gauges.

1. Open a new empty Flash file and import `machine-gauges.ai`. Use the same settings as you did for the machine import.

2. Click on the machine and navigate to **Modify | Break Apart**.

3. Click on the gauges and navigate to **Modify | Break Apart** again.

4. Click on the left gauge, navigate to **Modify | Break Apart**, and do the same for the right gauge. Now, the pointers are separate objects, as shown in the following screenshot:

5. Add a new layer and name it `gauge1`.

6. Click on the pointer in the left gauge, press *Ctrl/Cmd + X* to cut the pointer, select the new layer, and navigate to **Edit | Paste in Place** to paste the pointer on the same place of the canvas.

7. Select the pointer of the left gauge on the canvas and navigate to **Modify | Convert to Symbol**. Fill in the name `gauge1` and make sure **Movie Clip** is selected.

8. Double-click on the pointer; now you are inside the movie clip. At the top-left part, there's the name of the movie clip `gauge1`, next to `Scene 1`.

9. Right-click on the timeline of `frame 1` and choose **Create Motion Tween**. Click on **OK** for the question **Do you want to convert and create a tween?**

10. Click-and-drag the last frame to frame 20. The animation should last for 20 frames.

11. Select the **Free Transform Tool** in the **Tools** panel and move the rotation point to the center of the circle of the pointer, as shown in the following screenshot:

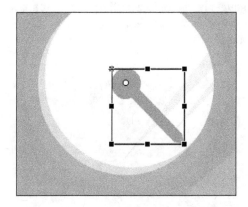

12. Now, click on the timeline, choose **Properties** panel, open the **Rotation** menu (if it's not already open), and fill in **Rotate: 1 time(s)**, as shown in the following screenshot:

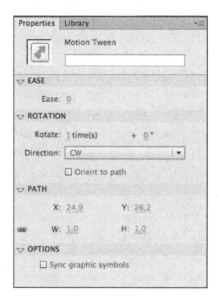

13. Save the file as `machine-gauges.fla`.

14. Press *Enter* to test the animation.

15. Click on `Scene 1` in the top-left corner to return to the root timeline.

16. Since the gauge is a movie clip, you can only test the animation when you use *Ctrl/Cmd + Enter*. The `machine-gauges.swf` file is automatically created.

You can create the animation for the second gauge exactly the same way. This animation should last for about 85 frames, so it's much slower than the first gauge.

Since we used movie clips, you don't see any animations in the root timeline. The animations are inside the timeline of the movie clips.

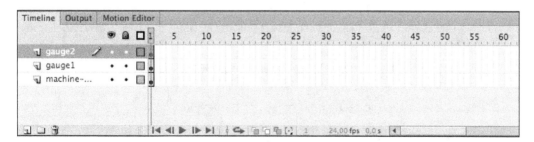

Let's create the third gauge's animation by performing the following steps:

1. Open a new empty Flash file and import `gauge3.ai`. Use the same settings that you used to import the machine. If you get the question **This file appears to be part of a sequence of images. Do you want to import all the image of the sequence?**, just click on **No**.

2. The pointer of this gauge should make a whole rotation in steps (and not smooth like the previous animations). In each step, the pointer should rotate 10 degrees. This means it takes 36 steps to complete a whole rotation (360 degrees).

3. Click on the gauge on the canvas and navigate to **Modify | Break Apart**.

4. Select the pointer and move it to a new layer.

5. Select the **Free Transform** tool and move the rotation point to the center of the circle of the pointer.

6. Right-click on `frame 10` in the new layer and choose **Insert Keyframe**. Open the **Transform** panel (*Ctrl/Cmd + T*) and fill in `10,0` for the **Rotate** option, as shown in the following screenshot:

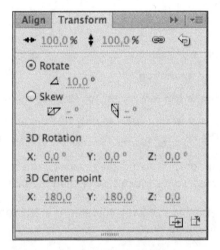

7. Right-click on `frame 20`, choose **Insert Keyframe**, open the **Transform** panel, and fill in `20` for **Rotate**.

8. Repeat this until you reached a rotation of 360 degrees. To be honest, this is not the most fun part.

9. Now, your last frame of the pointer layer is frame 360.

10. Right-click on `frame 360` in the `gauge3.ai` layer and choose **Insert Frame**.

11. Your timeline should look like the following screenshot:

12. Save the file as gauge3.fla, and use *Ctrl/Cmd + Enter* to create and view the .swf file.

It's time for the last animation. We're almost finished.

13. Open a new, empty Flash file and import gauge4.ai. This will be the gauge with the nervous pointer.

14. Click on the gauge on the canvas and navigate to **Modify | Break Apart**.

15. Select the pointer and move it to a new layer.

16. Right-click on the new layer on frame 1 and choose **Create Motion Tween**. Click **OK** to the question **Do you want to convert and create a tween?**.

17. Click-and-drag the last frame of the motion tween to frame 3.

18. Use the **Free Transform** tool to move the rotation point to the center of the circle of the pointer.

19. While the **Free Transform** tool is still selected, rotate the pointer a few degrees to the right, as shown in the following screenshot:

20. Right-click on frame 6 in the new layer and navigate to **Insert Keyframe | All**. Rotate the pointer back to the middle.

21. Right-click on frame 8 (not frame 9, that would make the animation too smooth) in the new layer and navigate to **Insert Keyframe | All**. Rotate the pointer back a few degrees to the left.

22. Right-click on `frame 11` in the new layer, navigate to **Insert Keyframe | All**, and rotate the pointer back to the middle.

23. Right-click on `frame 11` in the `gauge4.ai` layer and choose **Insert Frame**.

24. Save the file as `gauge4.fla` and use *Ctrl/Cmd + Enter* to create and view the `.swf` file. It is shown in the following screenshot:

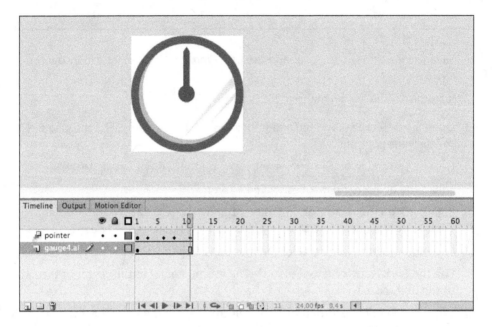

Objective complete – mini debriefing

We created all the animations for our prezi with Adobe Flash Professional. We used the `.ai` files for input and created different kinds of animations. We created motion tweens, frame-by-frame animations, and animations in movie clips.

Now, everything is finished to create our prezi.

Classified intel

We created a single file for every animation. It's also possible to create one file with all the animations in it. Most of the time this is more complicated. Also, with different files, you are more flexible in Prezi if you want to change something.

If you're already familiar with Flash, you could use separate movie clips for every animation and put them together in one file. Movie clips have their own timeline, which means that the cloud animations are not dependent on each other. The first cloud could start over again before the last cloud is finished. This makes your animations less predictable and, therefore, more real.

Putting it all together in Prezi

We have the illustrations and the animations ready. Now, we can put everything together in Prezi.

We are going to perform the following steps:

1. Open a new prezi.
2. Insert all the illustrations and animations and put them in the right place.
3. Add texts in Prezi.
4. Add a path.

Prepare for lift off

Open a new prezi, choose the blank template, and delete all the objects on the canvas. Make sure your canvas is completely empty.

Engage thrusters

1. Navigate to **Insert** | **From file** and insert `pipes.swf` on the canvas.
2. Insert `machine.swf`, `machine-gauges.swf`, `gauge3.swf`, and `gauge4.swf`. Then, scale them to the right format and put everything at the right location, as shown in the following screenshot:

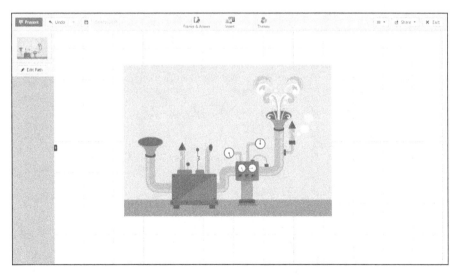

Now, let's change the background color. The light blue color of our illustration is 191, 231, and 241 in RGB colors.

3. Navigate to **Themes | Customize Current Theme**, choose **Advanced**, and fill in 191, 231, 241 for **Background Color**, as shown in the following screenshot:

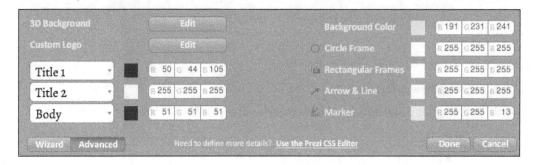

Maybe the light blue color you can see is not the exact color of the background of the illustration. It's better to remove the color from pipes.swf by performing the following steps:

1. Open pipes.fla in Adobe Flash Professional again. Click on the light blue background and press *Delete*. You can also choose a different background color.

2. Save the file and press *Ctrl/Cmd + Enter* to regenerate the .swf file.

3. Return to Prezi, remove pipes.swf, and insert the new pipes.swf file.

4. Right-click on the new pipes.swf file and choose **Send to Back** to put in to the background.

Maybe you have to rearrange a few objects. Now, add all the other illustrations and put them on the canvas. Copy and paste the hearts, scale them, and put as many in your prezi as you like.

Your prezi could now look similar to the following screenshot:

The next step is to add the text. All text is added in prezi to make it as flexible as possible.

We wrote down our story in the first task of this project. Use these texts in your prezi.
Of course, choose a nice font for your texts.

The last step to create this prezi is creating the path. Make a nice flow and don't forget to zoom out in the last path step. Use invisible frames.

The following are a few steps in the path:

- ▶ The following is path step 1:

- ▶ The following is path step 4:

- ▶ The following is path step 9:

▸ The following is path step 17:

▸ The following is path step 18:

▸ The following is path step 20:

Objective complete – mini debriefing

In this task, we only had to assemble our presentation in Prezi. All the illustrations and animations were already finished. After putting everything together, we added texts, and finally added a path to our prezi.

Classified intel

Of course, you can add more details similar to gear wheels in the machine or other nice objects.

Mission accomplished

We started this project with one main idea and created the story for it first. Then, we searched for a great illustration to visualize our idea.

In the Adobe Illustrator, we divided the illustration into smaller pieces—some as static images, others to be used for animation in the Adobe Flash Professional. We created animations in Flash, such as motion tweens, frame-by-frame animations, and animations in movie clips.

When every single image and animation was finished, we started building our prezi. We inserted the artwork and animations, added text, and created a path.

Our really cool animated prezi was finished and looked as shown the following screenshot:

A Hotshot challenge

In this project, you learned enough to create your own animations now. Think of a nice project to create animations for and get lost in Flash!

For instance, pimp up your prezumé (but remember, don't overdo it).

Project 9

More Interactivity with the Prezi Player API

With the Prezi Player API, you can communicate with your embedded prezi on a website using JavaScript code. The API gives you lots of possibilities for more interactivity with your prezis.

An **Application Programming Interface** (**API**) is a set of programming instructions to access a specific application. A software company releases its API to give developers the opportunity to communicate with their software. This way, programmers don't have to start from scratch; they can use the functions already written by the software company. For example, an automatic Twitter plugin on your website is created by a developer by using the Twitter API.

The status of the Prezi Player API is alpha. Check `prezi.github.io/prezi-player/` for the latest updates.

Mission briefing

In this project, we'll be creating a menu on a website to navigate through our embedded prezi. We'll be using HTML and CSS for the menu and we'll be using JavaScript to create the interactivity.

The prezi we'll be using in this project is *The world of bees* from *Project 3, I Want to Use Prezi For My Lessons*. Using the menu, the user can jump straight to a specific item and he gets a good overview about the content of the prezi.

You can choose whether the user is also allowed to freely navigate the prezi with the mouse or if they should use the the navigation menu.

You'll find the project at www.prezihotshot.com, where you can try the navigation yourself. If you don't want to type the code yourself or if you're afraid of making typos you can right click the webpage, select **View Source** and copy the code.

The following screenshot shows the overview of the prezi, which is also the starting point when you view the webpage:

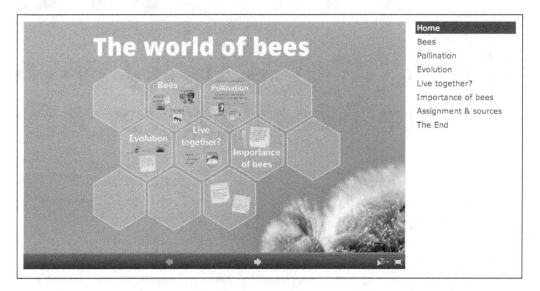

Here, we clicked on the menu item **Evolution** to zoom into that specific subject automatically, as shown in the following screenshot:

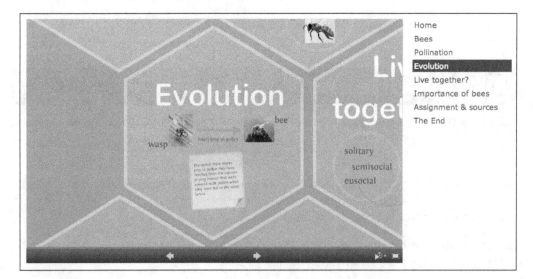

Why is it awesome?

Of course, Prezi itself is pretty cool, but if you can give the user more control over the prezi, that'll be brilliant!

Using a navigation menu to control a prezi is just an example of the possibilities of the Prezi Player API. The API provides functions for the following:

- ▸ Querying meta information, such as the title
- ▸ Querying actual information, such as the current step number or object ID
- ▸ Subscribing to changes in this information (callbacks)
- ▸ Moving around by jumping to an exact step or object, or moving to the previous or next step, starting autoplay, and so on

The possibilities of using the API are nonlinear storytelling, a chat room to discuss a prezi, syncing a prezi with a video, and interaction with the outside world by using location, gestures or sound.

In this project, we'll create a menu to navigate through our prezi by using HTML, CSS, and JavaScript, a great application of the Prezi Player API and very useful.

Your Hotshot objectives

The major tasks to complete this project are as follows:

- ▸ Embedding the prezi
- ▸ Creating the menu
- ▸ Making it work
- ▸ Creating a submenu

Mission checklist

To complete this project, you don't really need knowledge about HTML, CSS, or JavaScript, but of course it helps a lot if you have it.

I'll try to explain this project as simply as possible, because most Prezi users are not used to HTML, CSS, or JavaScript. You could use a (**What You See Is What You Get**) **WYSIWYG** HTML editor such as Adobe Dreamweaver, but you can also use a simple text editor such as Notepad. If you use a WYSIWYG editor, you have to work in code view. If you don't like code at all, you better skip this project.

You can find all documentation about the Prezi Player API at `prezi.github.io/prezi-player/`. The status of this API is alpha, so your code may clash with an update. Join the Prezi Player API mailing list to stay up to date.

You can make an online reference in your JavaScript code by using the following code:

```
<script src="http://prezi.github.io/prezi-
    player/lib/PreziPlayer/prezi_player.js"></script>
```

You can also download the JavaScript library at `prezi.github.io/prezi-player/getit.html`.

Embedding the prezi

Our first task in this exciting project is to embed our prezi in a webpage. So, first we need an empty webpage.

Prepare for lift off

Open your favorite HTML editor and open a new empty HTML page. Make sure you are working in the code view.

If you use a simple text editor, you can type the following code:

```
<html>
<head>
<title>The world of bees</title>
</head>
<body>
</body>
</html>
```

Save your file as `world-of-bees.html`.

Adobe Dreamweaver (and most other HTML editors) add additional code to your page as you can see in the next screenshot. The previous code gives you a better HTML page, but it's not necessary for the page to work.

In the following information box, you can find some extra information about HTML and CSS:

HTML is the abbreviation for HyperText Markup Language and is the main language used to create webpages. HTML elements consist of tags and mostly come in pairs such as `<h1></h1>` or `<body></body>`. The first tag in a pair is the start tag and the second tag is the end tag, also known as opening tags and closing tags. Between these tags, you will write text or other tags.

In 1989, Tim Berners-Lee invented the World Wide Web at CERN and he developed the first version of HTML in 1990.

CSS means Cascading Style Sheets and is the style language for your webpage. In the beginning, both content and design were written in HTML. With the introduction of CSS, the content was separated from the design. HTML should be used for the content and semantic structure of your webpage and CSS for the presentation elements such a layout, colors, and fonts.

Engage thrusters

Now, we have to embed our prezi in the webpage. Maybe you have done this before using the Embed option at `Prezi.com`, but now we'll be using the Prezi Player API for it.

First, we have to add the JavaScript library of the API to our webpage. We could download the library, store it local, and make a reference to it, but it's easier to point to the online library.

Add the following code between the `<body>` and `</body>` tags of your webpage:

```
<script src="http://prezi.github.io/prezi-
    player/lib/PreziPlayer/prezi_player.js"></script>
```

Now, we have our reference to JavaScript library and we can actually use it.

Add the following code:

```
<script type="text/javascript">
var player = new PreziPlayer('prezi-player', {
  preziId: "7iob-larbvwr",
  width: 800,
height: 500,
controls: true,
explorable: true
});
</script>
```

The `preziId` in this piece of code is very important and points to the specific prezi. If you use the code in this example, you'll load my prezi **The world of bees**. If you want to load your own prezi, perform the following steps:

1. First find the URL of your prezi at `Prezi.com`. Open your prezi online and have a look at the address bar of your browser. The URL of my prezi is `http://prezi.com/7iob-larbvwr/prezi-hotshot-world-of-bees-9/`.

2. The code right after `prezi.com` is your `preziId` that you have to use in your own code. In my example, it's `7iob-larbvwr`.

3. The `width` and `height` in this code example are 800 and 500 pixels. You can change this numbers yourself. Default values are 640 pixels for `width` and 480 pixels for `height`.

4. The parameter `controls` is set to `true` to show the progress bar and the next and previous buttons in the prezi on the webpage. If you don't want to show the controls, you can leave this code out or set it to `false`.

5. The parameter `explorable` is also set to `true` to allow the user to freely navigate through your prezi with mouse or touchpad. If you don't want this, you can leave this code out or set it to `false`.

   We are almost ready to view our prezi on the webpage. We have to make a reference to a HTML tag to make our prezi visible.

6. Add the following code above the JavaScript, just under the `<body>` tag:

   ```
   <div id="prezi-player"></div>
   ```

   The value for the `id` should be exactly the same as the value used to create a new PreziPlayer. Here, we used `prezi-player`.

Now, the full code between the `<body>` and `</body>` is as follows:

```
<div id="prezi-player"></div>

<script src="http://prezi.github.io/prezi-
    player/lib/PreziPlayer/prezi_player.js"></script>

<script type="text/javascript">
var player = new PreziPlayer('prezi-player', {
preziId: "7iob-larbvwr",
width: 800,
height: 500,
controls: true,
explorable: true
});
</script>
```

Make sure your HTML page is saved and open it in your browser. You should have a working Internet connection because we have a reference to an online source.

The Prezi Player API documentation says opening a HTML file directly in the browser will not work, but as long as you are not using callbacks, it will work. You might want to use callbacks if you want the menu to highlight depending on the path step in the prezi. Then, you'll have two-way communication and the HTML file should be online to make it work. In our examples, we won't be using callbacks.

Opening your HTML page in your browser gives you the result shown in the next screenshot:

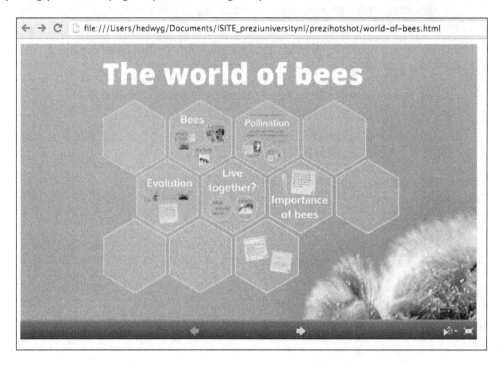

In the next information box, you'll find some extra information about JavaScript.

JavaScript is a programming language used to communicate with web browsers. Commonly, it's used on the client side to interact with the user, control the browser, and communicate asynchronously.

Don't confuse JavaScript with Java. JavaScript was developed by Netscape and is always used in combination with another language (such as HTML and CSS). Java was developed by Sun Microsystems and is an **Object Oriented Programming (OOP)** Language. With Java, you can develop standalone applications and no other language is required. Java code needs to be compiled (translated to machine language). JavaScript code can be used *as it is*; the browser can read the JavaScript directly. JavaScript is easier to learn than Java.

Objective complete – mini debriefing

In this task, we embedded our prezi on a webpage using the Prezi Player JavaScript library. First, we made a reference to the library. Then, we loaded the prezi into our webpage. We used a `<div>` tag to make the prezi visible in the browser. The next step is to add a menu to our webpage.

Classified intel

If you are not a programmer, but you like the things we are explaining here and want to learn more about coding, take a look at one of these sites:

- www.codecademy.com
- www.codeschool.com
- teamtreehouse.com

Creating the menu

Let's use HTML and CSS to create a nice menu on our webpage.

Engage thrusters

Return to your HTML editor. First, we'll create a menu with plain HTML. We use an unordered list for this.

In the code, we place it after the <div> for the embedded prezi, as shown in the following code:

```
<ul>
    <li>Home</li>
    <li>Bees</li>
    <li>Pollination</li>
    <li>Evolution</li>
    <li>Live together?</li>
    <li>Importance of bees</li>
    <li>Assignment & sources</li>
    <li>The End</li>
</ul>
```

When we look at our webpage, we can see that our menu is underneath our prezi. We want to position it on the right side of our prezi. We can solve this with CSS as shown in the following screenshot:

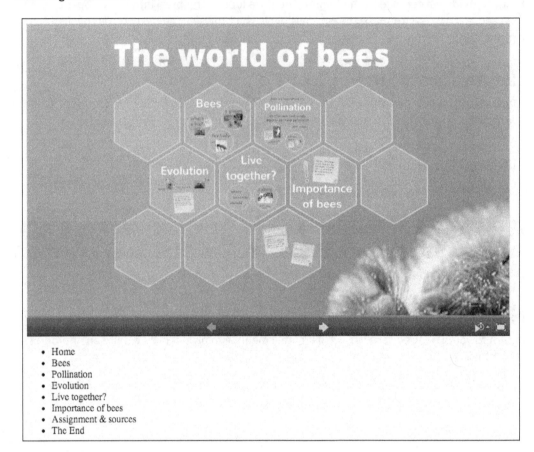

Next, we'll place the list in a `<div>` tag so that we can position the menu later with CSS. We'll also add an ID for the `<div>` tag and an ID for the `<ul>` tag. We'll create hyperlinks of the menu items with `<a href=""></a>`. For now, these hyperlinks are empty because we will use JavaScript to make the hyperlinks communicate with the prezi. However, we do need these hyperlinks to design our menu with CSS, as shown in the following code:

```
<div id="menu">
<ul id="nav">
        <li><a href="">Home</a></li>
        <li><a href="">Bees</a></li>
        <li><a href="">Pollination</a></li>
        <li><a href="">Evolution</a></li>
        <li><a href="">Live together?</a></li>
```

```
          <li><a href="">Importance of bees</a></li>
          <li><a href="">Assignment & sources</a></li>
          <li><a href="">The End</a></li>
    </ul>
    </div>
```

Our next step is to write the CSS code to design and position our menu. We have already created IDs that we'll refer to.

We will write our CSS code in the `<head></head>` part, just above the `</head>` tag. First we'll write the `<style></style>` code in the `<head></head>` section, as shown in the following code:

```
<head>
<title>The world of bees</title>
<style type="text/css">
</style>
</head>
```

We can add our CSS code between the `<style>` and `</style>` tags. We used the following code:

```
#prezi-player {
  width: 800px;
  float: left;
  margin-left: 20px;
}
#menu {
  width: 250px;
  margin-left: 800px;
  font-family: Verdana, Geneva, sans-serif;
}
#nav {
  list-style-type: none;
}
#nav li a {
  display: block;
  color: #333;
  padding: 3px;
  margin-bottom: 3px;
  text-decoration: none;
}
#nav li a:hover {
  background-color: #333;
  color: #fff;
}
```

Of course, we will not give a full CSS course here, but some explanations about CSS might be appropriate.

In CSS, you reference to an `id` with `#`. The code for `#prezi-player` gives the prezi the space for its width of 800 pixels. The code `float: left` lets you position to two `div` next to each other so that the menu can be positioned right next to the prezi.

The menu has a width of 250 pixels and a position of 800 pixels from the left side of the screen (`margin-left: 800px`). We removed the bullets from the list with the code `list-style-type: none`. The design of the menu is done in the code `#nav li a`.

When you move your mouse over the hyperlinks of the menu, a dark gray bar becomes visible for that specific menu item and the text will turn white. This is done with the code `#nav li a:hover`.

You can view the result of adding the CSS code in the following screenshot:

Objective complete – mini debriefing

In this task, we created our menu that we will use to communicate with our prezi. First, we created a plain unordered HTML list. With CSS, we designed this menu to something better looking and positioned it at the right side of the prezi.

Now, we have all the elements ready to add the JavaScript code.

Classified intel

You can also do other great stuff with CSS. In this example, we kept our menu simple and plain because we like that. If you want to get lost in CSS, try CSS transitions and transformations with CSS3.

Making it work

We embedded a prezi and created a menu. Now, let these two communicate with each other.

In the documentation of the Prezi Player API, there's a full API reference with all the functions you can use. To give you an idea, some functions with a short explanation are given here. This is not the full list.

- ▸ `.getStepCount()` : This returns the number of the steps of the prezi
- ▸ `.getCurrentStep()`: This returns the actual step number
- ▸ `.getTitle()`: This returns the title of the prezi
- ▸ `.flyToPreviousStep()`: This moves the prezi to the previous step
- ▸ `.flyToNextStep()`: This moves the prezi to the next step
- ▸ `.flyToStep(number)`: This moves the prezi to the number you provide
- ▸ `.play(milliseconds)`: This starts autoplaying the prezi
- ▸ `.pause(milliseconds)`: This is same as `.play()`, but pauses if prezi is already playing and starts autoplaying if not playing
- ▸ `.stop()`: This stops autoplaying the prezi

Prepare for lift off

It is important to know that developers start counting with 0.

Engage thrusters

For our project, we will be using just one API function: `.flyToStep()`. This function moves your prezi to the number you provide between the brackets. So, first find out which path step numbers belong to each menu item. But be aware! Developers start counting with 0, which means we have to subtract each number with 1. For example, in our prezi menu item **Importance of bees** is path number 21. This means we have to use 20 in our code.

The easiest way to add the code to your HTML is using the following code in your hyperlink:

```
javascript:player.flyToStep(0)
```

Copy-and-paste it in each hyperlink code between the quotes and change the number of the path step. The following is the new code for our menu:

```
<div id="menu">
  <ul id="nav">
  <li><a href="javascript:player.flyToStep(0)">Home</a></li>
  <li><a href="javascript:player.flyToStep(1)">Bees</a></li>
```

```
<li><a
  href="javascript:player.flyToStep(8)">Pollination</a></li>
<li><a href="javascript:player.flyToStep(13)">Evolution</a></li>
<li><a href="javascript:player.flyToStep(16)">Live
  together?</a></li>
<li><a href="javascript:player.flyToStep(20)">Importance of
  bees</a></li>
<li><a href="javascript:player.flyToStep(23)">Assignment &
  sources</a></li>
<li><a href="javascript:player.flyToStep(24)">The End</a></li>
</ul>
</div>
```

Save your new webpage and try it out!

 There's a much nicer way of programming this in JavaScript, but for our project this works perfectly and is easy to understand.

Objective complete – mini debriefing

In this task, we added the JavaScript code to our menu to communicate with our prezi. We used the function `.flyToStep()` for it. A full reference of functions of the Prezi Player API can be found in its documentation.

Classified intel

Now, our basic project is finished, play around with some parameters and functions. For example, leave out the parameters `controls` and `explorable` and see what happens.

Creating a submenu

In this task, we'll go just one step further. We'll create submenus for our menu items. The submenus let us navigate not only to the main subjects of the prezi, but also to the subparts.

Prepare for lift off

We want to keep our original file with the plain menu. Save your `world-of-bees.html` as `world-of-bees2.html` to create a new web page and continue working on the menu.

Engage thrusters

In our unordered list, we'll create new unordered lists for our submenus. Let's start with the first submenu for menu item **Bees**.

The following is the code of the new unordered list for the submenu:

```
<ul>
<li><a href="javascript:player.flyToStep(2)">what's a
  bee?</a></li>
<li><a href="javascript:player.flyToStep(4)">4 groups</a></li>
<li><a href="javascript:player.flyToStep(5)">bee body</a></li>
</ul>
```

Put this list between the `<li></li>` tags of the menu item **Bees**, just before the end tag `</li>`.

The code will look as shown in the following screenshot. Pay attention to the end tag `</li>` after the whole new sublist.

The webpage now looks like the following screenshot:

This code works immediately as you do not have to compile or upload it first. Maybe you want to change the design of the sublist, we will do that later. First, we'll add the other sublists to our menu.

Look at the following screenshot for the code of the complete menu.

```
36  <div id="prezi-player"></div>
37  <div id="menu">
38      <ul id="nav">
39          <li><a href="javascript:player.flyToStep(0)">Home</a></li>
40          <li><a href="javascript:player.flyToStep(1)">Bees</a>
41          <ul>
42              <li><a href="javascript:player.flyToStep(2)">what's a bee?</a></li>
43              <li><a href="javascript:player.flyToStep(4)">4 groups</a></li>
44              <li><a href="javascript:player.flyToStep(5)">bee body</a></li>
45          </ul>
46          </li>
47          <li><a href="javascript:player.flyToStep(8)">Pollination</a>
48          <ul>
49              <li><a href="javascript:player.flyToStep(9)">beekeepers</a></li>
50              <li><a href="javascript:player.flyToStep(10)">pollinator decline</a></li>
51          </ul>
52          </li>
53          <li><a href="javascript:player.flyToStep(13)">Evolution</a></li>
54          <li><a href="javascript:player.flyToStep(16)">Live together?</a>
55          <ul>
56              <li><a href="javascript:player.flyToStep(17)">solitary, semisocial, eusocial</a></li>
57              <li><a href="javascript:player.flyToStep(18)">colony</a></li>
58          </ul>
59          </li>
60          <li><a href="javascript:player.flyToStep(20)">Importance of bees</a></li>
61          <li><a href="javascript:player.flyToStep(23)">Assignment & sources</a></li>
62          <li><a href="javascript:player.flyToStep(24)">The End</a></li>
63      </ul>
```

The last thing that we want to change is the design of the submenu. We want to get rid of the bullets and we want to give the submenu a lighter background if we move the mouse over it.

In the CSS part, we add the following code to accomplish this:

```
#nav li li {
  list-style-type: none;
  margin-left: -24px;
}
#nav li li a:hover {
  background-color: #777;
  color: #fff;
}
```

By using `li li`, we can reference to the submenu instead of the main menu items, as shown in the following screenshot:

Objective complete – mini debriefing

In this task, we created submenus for our prezi by using nested unordered lists in the HTML code. We also added some CSS code to change to design of the submenus. The JavaScript code to communicate with the prezi was the same, except from the path step numbers.

Mission accomplished

In this project, we used the Prezi Player API to create more interactivity for our prezi. We embedded a prezi in a webpage, created a menu with HTML and CSS, and used JavaScript code to communicate with the prezi.

If you click on a menu item, the prezi flies immediately to the right path step. Besides the menu, you can give the user full control over the prezi, but you can also decide whether the menu is the only way to navigate through the prezi.

It might seem to you a difficult job to do in advance, but as you have seen, it's really easy.

A Hotshot challenge

If you like coding and are looking for a challenge, try the following. Now the menu items will be highlighted when you move your mouse over them, but wouldn't it be great if the menu item stays highlighted after you clicked it?

Also, if you move in the prezi to a specific path step, the corresponding menu item will be highlighted automatically. You have to use callbacks to accomplish this and it only works online or with a local webserver.

An example is at `prezi.com/manual/transitions-tutorial/`, created by developers of `Prezi.com`. Of course, you can have a look at the source code to learn how it was done.

Project 10

Creating an
Award-winning Prezi

On February 7, 2013, I received a newsletter from Prezi.com with an announcement for a contest. It said: Prezi + TED Contest. **TED** is a global set of conferences with the mission of spreading ideas, usually in the form of powerful talks (18 minutes or less). TED stands for Technology, Entertainment, and Design. Visit their website at www.ted.com.

By winning the contest, you could win a lifetime Pro license, but I didn't mind paying for my license. My agenda was pretty full and my kids were on their spring holidays.
So, I thought, "Hmmm... I don't know."

However, as an official Prezi expert, I felt I had to enter the competition. So, I went to the **Ideas Matter** page, read everything about it (yes, everything), and I decided I didn't have time for it.

However, the idea didn't let go of me. I chose a TED Talk, started working on a prezi, remained unsure whether to enter the competition till the last moment, and finally submitted my presentation just before the deadline.

Early in the morning of February 28, 2013, I got an e-mail from Prezi.com with the message, "On behalf of Prezi, congratulations! You have been chosen as a finalist in our Ideas Matter contest".

I was thrilled! I was just about to drive to Amsterdam to teach another prezi course, but I stepped out of the car, ran back into the house, and danced and yelled, "I'm a finalist!". My husband and kids thought I had gone crazy.

I had a big smile on my face and was very happy on the whole way to Amsterdam. This was it! I was a finalist in the *Ideas Matter* contest. This was what I was hoping for and I made it. This was enough for me.

However, it wasn't enough for the jury.

Later on that day, I heard that Chris Anderson, the curator of TED, and Peter Arvai, CEO of Prezi, chose me as the grand prize winner. I had won the contest!

I'll never forget that feeling. For me, it was the crowning glory of my work. Have a look at to the following screenshot:

Prezi + TED Contest

We've joined with TED Conferences to host an *Ideas Matter* contest. Create and submit a prezi inspired by one of five popular TED Talks.

Ten finalists will receive **lifetime Pro licenses**, and one grand prize winner will be **featured on both Prezi & TED's websites** as well as in the second edition of *Ideas Matter Spotlight*.

Ideas Matter Contest ›

Mission briefing

In this project, I will explain how I created the winning prezi IDENTITY for the Prezi + TED Contest, Ideas Matter.

I will start from the beginning of the assignment, what the assignment was exactly, and how I dealt with it. Next, I will try to explain, as much as possible, what my process was. I think taking time on the process is very important. Knowing how to design and use prezi is important, but taking time to find the key message is of greater importance.

Of course, I will also explain how I created the prezi. I will clarify some special effects for which I got lots of questions on how I did it.

Why is it awesome?

In this project, you will get a look through the eyes of the designer. How did the process go? What decisions were made? Was it well-structured or was there chaos? Was it all carefully planned or did you need some luck as well? How did you know a decision works?

I think it's interesting to share as much as I can so that you can learn from it.

Your Hotshot objectives

The major tasks to complete this project are as follows:

▸ Learning about the assignment

▸ Explaining the process

▸ Creating the prezi

▸ Special effects

Mission checklist

I used Adobe Illustrator and Flash to create some of the special effects in the prezi. For the process and thinking of the key message, I only used paper, a pen, and a highlighter.

Learning about the assignment

The assignment for the Prezi + TED Contest was easy and the steps were as follows:

1. Make a prezi that embodies the key messages of your chosen TED Talk.
2. Explain the prezi in a unique way.

The complete description of the assignment, as quoted at `prezi.com`, is as follows:

Choose a TED Talk as the starting point for a prezi that you design.

TED Talks are driven by ideas, and so are prezis. Audiences are inspired by presentations that focus on big ideas with the potential to spread, inspire others, and change the world. When ideas are visual, they are even more memorable.

This is where Prezi comes in. Our invitation to you: Make a prezi that embodies the key messages of your chosen TED Talk and explains them in a unique way.

The prezi was judged on the following criteria:

▶ **Creativity**: Whether or not the prezi reflects a truly creative effort, and the prezi is unique and beautiful

▶ **Clarity**: Whether or not the message and format of the prezi is clear, understandable, and accessible to a broad audience

▶ **Incorporation of TED Talk**: Whether or not the prezi clearly follows, and even illuminates, the speaker's theme and message

There were the following five TED Talks to choose from:

▶ Elizabeth Gilbert's "Your elusive creative genius"

▶ Bryan Stevenson's "We need to talk about an injustice"

▶ Chip Conley's "Measuring what makes life worthwhile"

▶ Sarah Kay's "If I should have a daughter..."

▶ Matthieu Ricard's "The habits of happiness"

Take a look at the following screenshot:

Engage thrusters

The first thing I did was watch all five TED Talks. I also printed the full transcripts and read them. I wanted to make the right decision on the TED Talk. For me, that was the first important decision in the whole design process. I had to choose the talk that had the most impact on me. I could only design a prezi when I understood the TED Talk completely and when my heart was touched by the message.

For me, this wasn't an easy decision and it actually took me several days. I kept watching and reading the talks, putting it away, thinking about it, and watching and reading the talks again.

All the TED talks were truly amazing, but the one that made the biggest impression on me was the TED Talk *We need to talk about an injustice* by Bryan Stevenson, a Human Rights lawyer in the United States. The following information can be found at `http://en.wikipedia.org/wiki/Bryan_Stevenson`:

> *Bryan A. Stevenson is the founder and Executive Director of the Equal Justice Initiative, a private, non-profit organization headquartered in Montgomery, Alabama, and is a professor at New York University School of Law. He has gained national acclaim for his work challenging bias against the poor and people of color in the criminal justice system. Stevenson has assisted in securing relief for dozens of condemned prisoners, advocated for poor people and developed community-based reform litigation aimed at improving the administration of criminal justice.*

When I made the decision for the TED talk of Bryan Stevenson, I watched the talk a few more times. I also printed the transcript in Dutch, my native language, because I wanted to know what the talk was about in every detail.

Objective complete – mini debriefing

My first task in the design contest was deciding which TED Talk I should choose. I didn't take this decision quickly. I watched all videos, read the transcripts, and thought it through. For me, it took several days. That's not necessary for you, but pay enough attention to the start off a new prezi. What exactly is the assignment? What's the goal, message, and audience?

Explaining the process

In this task, I will explain the process of designing that took place before I started working in Prezi.

Prepare for lift off

I printed a six-page transcript (about 4000 words) of Bryan Stevenson's TED Talk, both in English and Dutch, to fully understand it and to start working on it. Besides the printout, I used a highlighter and a pen.

Engage thrusters

This section is the most important part of the whole process.

I started reading the full transcript with a highlighter and a pen in my hand. I highlighted every word that seemed important to me and took notes in the margins. I distinguished between facts and the anecdotes that Bryan Stevenson told, because these were completely different kinds of information.

Bryan Stevenson told three stories in his speech. The first story was the story about his grandmother. The first paragraph of the story goes as follows:

> I grew up in a house that was the traditional African American home that was dominated by a matriarch, and that matriarch was my grandmother. She was tough, she was strong, she was powerful. She was the end of every argument in our family. She was the beginning of a lot of arguments in our family. She was the daughter of people who were actually enslaved. Her parents were born in slavery in Virginia in the '40s. She was born in 1880 and the experience of slavery very much shaped the way she saw the world.

The second story is about Rosa Parks. She was an African-American civil rights activist and known as the "first lady of civil rights" and "the mother of the freedom movement." On December 1, 1955, in Montgomery, Alabama, Parks refused to obey the bus driver's order that she should give up her seat in the colored section to a white passenger after the white section was filled.

Bryan Stevenson had the privilege to meet Rosa Parks when he was a young lawyer. Sometimes, Rosa Parks got together with some of her dearest friends and just talked with them. Bryan Stevenson was invited to just listen, which was very energizing and empowering to him.

The third story Bryan Stevenson told in his speech was about the young kids who must stand trial as an adult.

> And I was up too late one night and I starting thinking, well gosh, if the judge can turn you into something that you're not, the judge must have magic power. Yeah, Bryan, the judge has some magic power. You should ask for some of that. And because I was up too late, wasn't thinking real straight, I started working on a motion. And I had a client who was 14 years old, a young, poor black kid. And I started working on this motion, and the head of the motion was: "Motion to try my poor, 14-year-old black male client like a privileged, white 75-year-old corporate executive."

Though all these three stories are beautifully told and very impressive, I decided not to include the stories in the prezi for two reasons. The first reason was it's very difficult to visualize these stories in the right, respectful way. The second reason is that the prezi would be too long. I wanted only to take the key message and visualize this in a prezi. The prezi shouldn't be a copy of Bryan Stevenson's speech.

While looking through my highlighted words, I noticed I highlighted the word "identity" often. Some phrases were as follows:

> *TED has an identity.*

> *I think identity is very important.*

> *And so I want to talk about the power of identity.*

> *Well I believe that our identity is at risk.*

> *Because it's in that nexus that we actually begin to understand truly profound things about who we are.*

The last sentence does not contain the word "identity" but it's clearly about identity.

Bryan Stevenson started his talk with identity and he ended it with identity. According to me, *identity* was the most important word in his speech. Therefore, I decided the word *identity* would be the key of my prezi. I also wanted to start and end the prezi with this word, just like Bryan Stevenson had done in his speech.

I didn't know exactly how I would visualize and design it, so I started to play around with the word IDENTITY on paper. It didn't take me very long to see I wanted to put information about the speech in every letter of the word IDENTITY. I wanted to start the prezi inside this word, walking through every letter, and at the end, zooming out to reveal the whole word.

IDENTITY consists of eight letters, so I needed eight pieces of information. I went through my notes, puzzled with the pieces, and came to the following parts of the speech of Bryan Stevenson:

- Identity is really important. When we create the right kind of identity, we can say things to the world around us. When we get them to do things that they don't think they can do.
- Facts about (black) people in prison in the US:
    - **1972**: 300,000 people
    - **2012**: 2.3 million people
- One out of three black men between the ages 18 and 30 is in jail, in prison, on probation or parole.

- Mass detention, that is, in Bryan Stevenson's state Alabama, 34 percent of the black male population has permanently lost the right to vote.

- We have a system of justice that treats you much better if you're rich and guilty than if you're poor and innocent.

- It's 11 times more likely that someone will get the death penalty if the victim is white than if the victim is black, and 22 times more likely if the defendant is black and the victim white. Do they deserve to die? Do we deserve to kill people?

- We love innovation, technology, creativity, and entertainment. Those realities are shadowed by suffering, abuse, degradation, and marginalization.

- Each of us is more than the worst thing we've ever done. If somebody tells a lie, they're not just a liar. If somebody takes something that doesn't belong to them, they're not just a thief. Even if you kill someone, you're not just a killer.

- Equal Justice Initiative: The opposite of poverty is not wealth. The opposite of poverty is justice.

- Ultimately, you judge the character of a society, not by how they treat their rich and the powerful and the privileged, but by how they treat the poor, the condemned, the incarcerated. Because it's in that nexus that we actually begin to understand truly profound things about who we are.

Now, I could start building and testing what I wanted in Prezi. However, before I did that, I had a few more considerations that were important to me:

- I really wanted to share the key message of the prezi to show the importance of the subject and to add my small contribution

- I intentionally did not put any ads in the prezi to make sure the focus was on the message and not on my company, Prezi University

- The style I wanted was black and white, sober and clean, and no fancy colors

- I wanted to use all the new features of Prezi, such as audio, 3D backgrounds, and animations (just because I like these features so much) and I thought it was a good idea to try out these features for the contest

- I wanted to end the prezi with a tribute to Bryan Stevenson

Now, I was ready to start in the prezi.

Objective complete – mini debriefing

In this task, I explained my process of collecting information and setting up the concept of the prezi. These are the most important steps in the whole design process.

What I did is as follows:

- Print the transcript
- Read it very carefully while highlighting important words and taking notes in the margins
- Start brainstorming with the highlighted information and notes
- Decide the beginning and ending style of the prezi—the prezi should start with the word IDENTITY and should end with it
- Decide which information will be placed in the word IDENTITY
- Find out what pieces should go in which letter of the word IDENTITY

Classified intel

Another interesting thing to do when you have a bunch of text is to create a **wordle** out of it. This is a word cloud that gives greater prominence to words that appear more frequently in the source text.

One of the sites where you can create word clouds is `www.wordle.net`.

The following image is the world cloud of the transcript of Bryan Stevenson's speech:

Creating the prezi

In this task, I will explain how I created the prezi and how I made the other design decisions. Now that I had the basic idea for the prezi, I had to create this and find out if my concept was working. From experience, I know that if you start working on your concept in Prezi, other great ideas pop up because you get into a creative mode.

Engage thrusters

Creating a prezi doesn't always go in a logical order. While you are working, you'll get new ideas, and sometimes, it's such a good idea that you want to try it out right away.

The very first thing I did was to put the word IDENTITY in it. I used a very bold font for it, **Open Sans Bold**, as shown in the following screenshot:

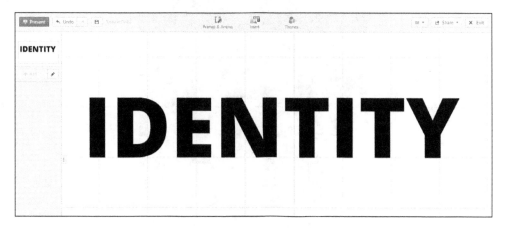

Then, I started filling the letters. The following screenshot shows the filled word:

I will show and explain each letter.

The letter **I** contains the text **IDENTITY IS REALLY IMPORTANT**, two silhouettes with accompanying text and two voice-overs. The silhouettes are actually holes in the letter **I**. You can't do that with fonts, so the text in the prezi is **DENTITY** and the **I** letter (with silhouettes) is an `Illustrator` file. As the silhouettes are holes, you can see the background through the letter. Refer to the following screenshot:

The letter **D** contains facts about the black people in prison in the United States. The facts are about the United States, and putting these facts in a map of the United States is a great way to visualize it. It looked like a coincidence to me that the map of the United States fits perfectly in the letter D by turning it ninety degrees to the left. The result looks really nice. As I wanted to show some facts here; I used the infographic style for this. The information isn't displayed at once, but in a few steps and a few zooms.

The map of the United States was created in Adobe Illustrator as a completely white map on black background, and it was put in Prezi as a SWF file. It was amazing to see how the map fit in the letter **D**! Refer to the following screenshot:

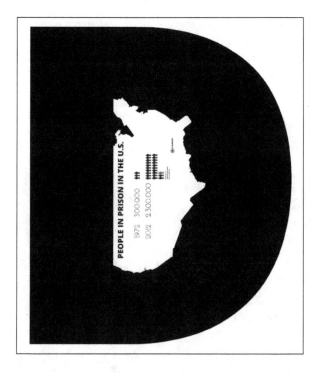

The following screenshot shows a close-up of the map:

In the letter **E**, I created a video with an infinite loop. I will explain in the next project how I created that video. On the top of the video, I inserted the text. As the video never stops and the text is on the top of it, it gives a very special effect. I got many questions about it. The video was of a man behind bars, who is looking at the viewer. This had a strong impact on the audience. Refer to the following screenshot:

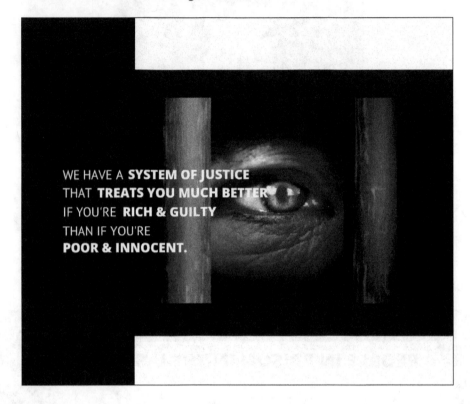

The letter **N** contains text and a Flash animation. I created a Flash animation from the text **kill?** to give the word even more impact.

I will not explain the Flash animation, because *Project 8*, *Let's Animate Your Prezi*, contains many examples of Flash animations. Refer to the following screenshot:

The following screenshot shows a close-up of the letter content of the letter **N**:

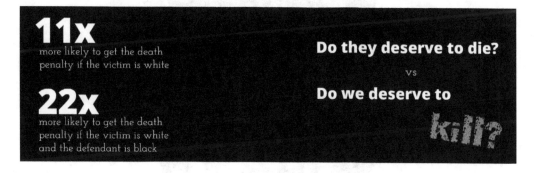

The letter **T** consists of two parts. The first part starts with **We love...**, and on the top of this the text, **But these realities are shadowed by...**. It's done by Prezi's Fade-in animation. Refer to the following screenshot:

In the following screenshot, you can see the images that are put on the top of the words **innovation**, **technology**, **entertainment**, and **creativity**:

The second letter **I** is *just* a text with voice-overs. However. for me, this was a very important quote of Bryan Stevenson. I think these sentences are very powerful and every time I hear Bryan Stevenson say these sentences, I get goosebumps. Take a look at the following screenshot:

The second **T** shows another Fade-in animation. It seems that the word **WEALTH** changes into **JUSTICE,** but actually, it's put on the top of it. The secret is that the word **JUSTICE** is put in a black rectangle that completely covers the word **WEALTH** if it becomes visible.

The following screenshot shows the first phase of the Fade-in animation:

The following screenshot shows the second phase:

In the following screenshot, I moved the rectangle with the word **JUSTICE** a bit to the upper-right corner so that you can see how it was done. In Prezi, the words are exactly on top of each other, so it seems that the first word changes to the second word.

The last letter contains text and a voice-over. Though the content is special, there's nothing special about this letter. Refer to the following screenshot:

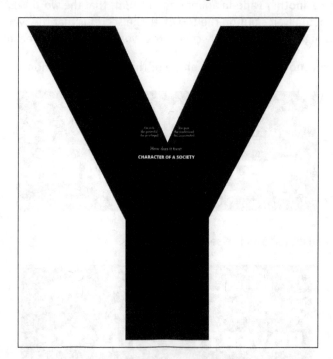

The following screenshot shows a close-up of the letter **Y**:

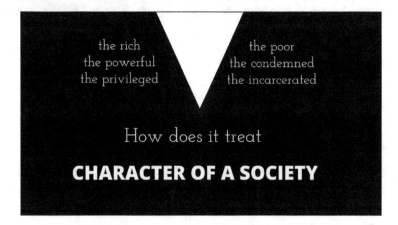

After moving through all the letters with the content, I created a big zoom-out slide that reveals my tribute to Bryan Stevenson, a picture of him on the stage giving his incredible TED Talk. It was not only the picture that is my tribute to him, but I also put the last words of his speech as voice-over in the prezi, including the big applause he received. Take a look at the following screenshot:

Objective complete – mini debriefing

In this task, I explained the most important design decisions and how they were made in Prezi. I did not explain every small step. **IDENTITY** was the basis for the prezi and all of the content was in the letters of **IDENTITY**. After going through the letters, there's a big zoom-out slide with a tribute to Bryan Stevenson.

In the next task, I'll explain the special effects of the prezi.

Creating special effects

In this task, I will explain the following three special effects of the prezi:

- ▸ Three-dimensional background
- ▸ Voice-overs
- ▸ Video of the eye

Prepare for lift off

To create voice-overs, you'll need sound editing software. I used Audacity (`audacity.sourceforge.net`) for it. To create the video of the eye looking through the prison bars, you'll need Adobe Flash Professional and, depending on the file format, a converter. I bought the original video available at `iStockphoto.com`.

Engage thrusters

Let's start with how I used a 3D background in the prezi.

Using a 3D background

What I often do while designing a prezi is scroll through a stock photo site, such as `iStockphoto.com`. I type in one or two keywords and search for the inspirational pictures. These pictures give me new thoughts and new ideas.

This was exactly what I was doing while working on my prezi for the Prezi + TED contest. I searched the terms prison, barbed wire, and black and white and found the following image:

The image was beautiful, simple, and perfect for my presentation. I loved the blurred background and the simple detail of the barbed wire.

If you are not sure if an image works for your presentation, you can try it out with a comp, which is a free image of low resolution, with a watermark just to test the image. At `iStockphoto.com`, you can click on **Download a Comp**, as shown in the following screenshot:

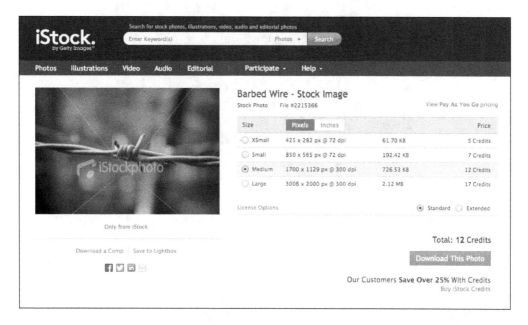

Before I put this picture as 3D background in the prezi, I felt that the prezi wasn't finished. Take a look at the following two images and you will you know what I mean. The prezi needed something else, and the three-dimensional background was the missing element.

The following screenshot shows the prezi without a three-dimensional background:

The following screenshot shows what the prezi looks like with the three-dimensional background:

I added the barbed wire image as the three-dimensional background by navigating to **Themes | Customize Current Theme**.

A three-dimensional background moves with a different speed while zooming in and out and gives you the illusion of three dimension. The three-dimensional background does not only give you 'an illusion'. It gives you an illusion of three-dimensions. It's hard to precisely predict what you will see in the three-dimension background. In my prezi, it was even better than I could imagine. When you move through the prezi, you'll see just a small piece of the picture every time because you are "looking through" the word **IDENTITY**. So, you don't see the whole image of the barbed wire, but you definitely get the feeling of it. You'll only see a glimpse of the barbed wire when moving from letter to letter, and it isn't visible inside the letter where the content is. At the end, you'll see the barbed wire in the background, but you won't be able to see the center of the picture, the "most dangerous part." The photo of Bryan Stevenson is covering this part, and I think that makes
the effect really strong.

In the following screenshot, you can see five snapshots of moving through the prezi while seeing a glimpse of the barbed wire:

Using voice-overs

You can add sound to your prezi by using background music and or voice-overs. As my prezi was inspired by a speech, I used parts of the original speech as voice-overs in the prezi.

Luckily, TED provides not only the transcript of the speech but also the audio file. You can download it from the site ted.com, as shown in the following screenshot:

I used the software Audacity to cut the audio file. Perform the following steps:

1. In Audacity, navigate to **File** | **Open** to open the audio file.

2. Then, select the part of the audio you want to cut; just click-and-drag in the audio file. As an example, I selected a part of 2 minutes in the next image. You can fine-tune this at the bottom of the screen. When you click on the **Play** button, you can listen to your selected part, as shown in the following screenshot:

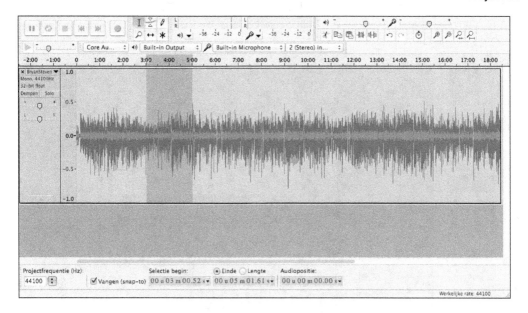

3. When you are satisfied with your selected part of the audio file, you can cut that part with the *Ctrl/Cmd + X* keys, open a new audio file with the *Ctrl/Cmd + N* keys, and paste it with the *Ctrl/Cmd + V* keys.

4. Navigate to **File** | **Export** to save your new audio file as **MP3**.

5. You can also add effects such as Fade-in and Fade-out. Select the part of the audio file you want to **fade-in** or **fade-out**, usually a small part of the beginning or the end of the sound file, and navigate to **Effects** | **Fade-in** or **Effects** | **Fade-out**.

6. Test your changed audio file and export it as MP3.

Now, you can add your audio file to your prezi. You can add it to a path step by performing the following steps:

1. First, click on the path step in the left sidebar of the Prezi editor.

2. Then, right-click on the **Add Voice-over to Path Step** option or navigate to **Insert** | **Add Voice-over to Path Step**.

3. Find your audio file and open it to add it to the specific path step.

In the following screenshot, you can see the path steps that contain audio files; they are denoted by the small musical notes symbol in the left sidebar:

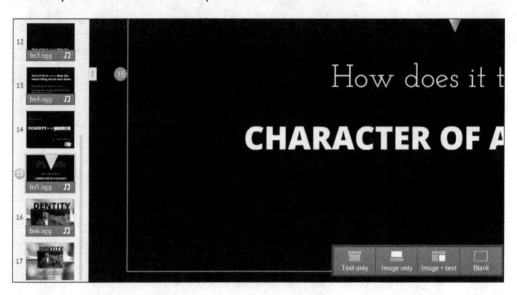

Creating the video of the eye

I was asked many questions about the always-moving eye in the prezi IDENTITY. I will explain how you can do it. Take a look at the following screenshot:

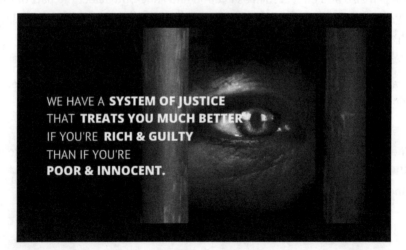

I bought the video from iStockphoto.com and downloaded the video in 640 x 360 pixels resolution and in the MOV format. The file size was 25.7 MB. It's ok if your video is in another file format.

Before you can use the video in Flash, you have to convert it to FLV. I used Adobe Media Encoder for it, but you can also use the tools available at www.zamzar.com or any tool. Perform the following steps:

1. In Adobe Media Encoder, navigate to **File | Add Source**, search the video file, and open it.

2. For the **Output File** option, select **FLV** and **Match Source Attributes (High Quality)**. You could also choose another output resolution, depending on the source resolution, but it makes no sense to select a resolution higher than the source file.

3. Navigate to **File | Start Queue** (or use the **Play** button) to start the conversion. My output file is 1.5 MB and that's fine. Refer to the following screenshot:

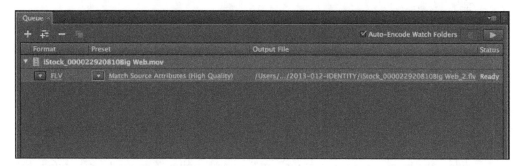

Now, open a new Flash file in Adobe Flash Professional and perform the following steps:

1. Navigate to **File | Import | Import Video**.

2. A dialog box opens. Click on the **Browse** button, search for the FLV file, and select it.

3. Select the **Embed FLV in SWF and play in timeline** option and click on **Next**, as shown in the following screenshot:

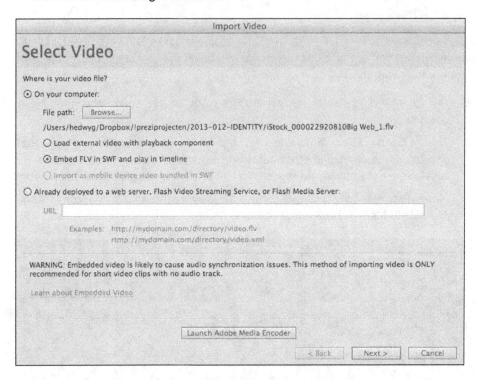

4. Select the **Place instance on stage** and **Expand timeline if needed** options and click on **Next** again, as shown in the following screenshot:

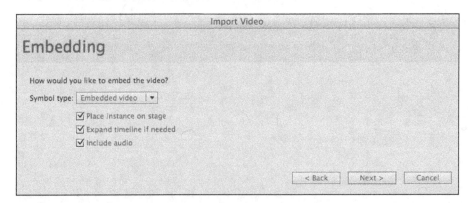

5. Click on **Finish**.

6. Click on the movie and press the *Ctrl/Cmd* + *I* keys to find the width and height of the movie.

7. Navigate to **Modify | Document** and change the dimensions accordingly so that the stage has the same size as the movie, as shown in the following screenshot:

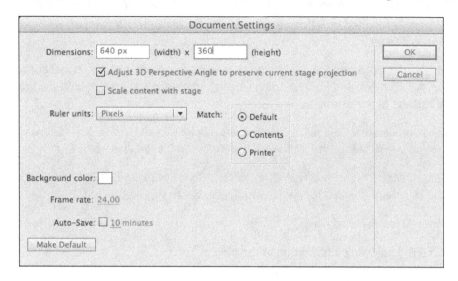

8. Save your Flash file and press *Ctrl/Cmd + Enter* to publish your movie. A SWF file will be created.

The SWF file contains the never-ending video and you are ready to use it in Prezi now. The file size of my SWF file was 1.3 MB. Take a look at the following screenshot:

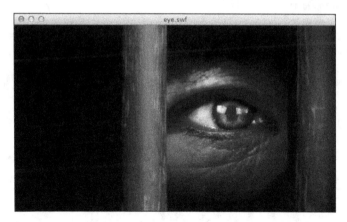

Objective complete – mini debriefing

In this task, I explained how the three special effects used in my prezi were created. The effects are: an image of a barbed wire as a three-dimensional background, the voice-over used in the prezi, and the looping eye video.

Mission accomplished

In this project, I explained how I created my winning prezi IDENTITY for the TED-Prezi contest, Ideas Matter.

I told you about my preparation, what I did to familiarize myself with the subject of the TED Talk, how I got creative, and how I made my design decisions. I also explained the most technical aspects of the prezi.

I hope I showed you that I did not create this prezi in just an afternoon. It was hard work, sometimes very frustrating, and it took a lot of time, but I loved every bit of it!

> *"Hedwyg's Prezi repurposed inspiring parts of Bryan's talk and added imaginative depth to spread the idea for a wider audience. We're very impressed."*

> —*Peter Arvai, CEO Prezi Inc.*

You can find the following information at the blog of Prezi.

> *Hedwyg's prezi not only echoed Bryan Stevenson's urgent words, but it combined his message with images, infographics, and moving pictures to give the talk even more depth and reach a wider audience. Needless to say, we're proud to see Hedwyg's prezi featured on the TED blog.*

The following image shows Chris Anderson, the curator of TED, and Peter Arvai, CEO of Prezi, showing the prezi IDENTITY:

A Hotshot challenge

All of the TED Talks have great content and contain great stories. It's an ideal way to develop your prezi and design skills by building a prezi inspired by a TED Talk.

So, find your favorite TED Talk, watch it over and over again, print the transcript, start highlighting, take notes, brainstorm, think, design, think again, and build a great prezi!

Index

About Packt Publishing

Packt, pronounced 'packed', published its first book "*Mastering phpMyAdmin for Effective MySQL Management*" in April 2004 and subsequently continued to specialize in publishing highly focused books on specific technologies and solutions.

Our books and publications share the experiences of your fellow IT professionals in adapting and customizing today's systems, applications, and frameworks. Our solution based books give you the knowledge and power to customize the software and technologies you're using to get the job done. Packt books are more specific and less general than the IT books you have seen in the past. Our unique business model allows us to bring you more focused information, giving you more of what you need to know, and less of what you don't.

Packt is a modern, yet unique publishing company, which focuses on producing quality, cutting-edge books for communities of developers, administrators, and newbies alike. For more information, please visit our website: www.packtpub.com.

Writing for Packt

We welcome all inquiries from people who are interested in authoring. Book proposals should be sent to author@packtpub.com. If your book idea is still at an early stage and you would like to discuss it first before writing a formal book proposal, contact us; one of our commissioning editors will get in touch with you.

We're not just looking for published authors; if you have strong technical skills but no writing experience, our experienced editors can help you develop a writing career, or simply get some additional reward for your expertise.

Instant Prezi Starter [Instant]

ISBN: 978-1-84969-702-6   Paperback: 56 pages

A user-friendly, step-by-step introductory guide to using Prezi, a web-based presentation aplication program ideal for engaging your audience

1. Learn something new in an Instant! A short, fast, focused guide delivering immediate results.

2. Amaze your audience and keep them engaged during your presentations with Prezi.

3. Learn with the help of practical resources for awesome examples and inspiration.

Mastering Prezi for Business Presentations

ISBN: 978-1-84969-302-8   Paperback: 258 pages

Engage your audience visually with stuning Prezi presentation designs and be the envy of your colleagues who use PowerPoint

1. Turns anyone already using Prezi into a master of both design and delivery.

2. Illustrated throughout with easy to follow screenshots and some live Prezi examples to view online.

3. Written by Russell Anderson-Williams, one of the fourteen experts hand-picked by Prezi.

Please check **www.PacktPub.com** for information on our titles

Building Impressive Presentations with impress.js

ISBN: 978-1-84969-648-7   Paperback: 124 pages

Design stunning presentations with dynamic visuals and 3D transitions that will captivate your colleagues

1. Create presentations inside the infinite canvas of modern web browsers.

2. Build presentations that work anywhere, any time, and on any device.

3. Build dynamic presentations with rotation, scaling, transforms, and 3D effects.

Instant HTML5 Presentations How-to [Instant]

ISBN: 978-1-78216-478-4   Paperback: 64 pages

Create beautiful and functional presentations using the reveal.js library, HTML5, and CSS3

1. Learn something new in an Instant! A short, fast, focused guide delivering immediate results.

2. Create presentations using HTML5 and run them straight from your browser.

3. Easily publish presentations on your website by using modern web technologies.

Please check **www.PacktPub.com** for information on our titles

www.ingramcontent.com/pod-product-compliance
Lightning Source LLC
LaVergne TN
LVHW062311060326
832902LV00013B/2160